Door-to-Door Millionaire: Secrets of Making the Sale

Lenny Gray

ISBN: 1-4820-6098-1
ISBN-13: 9781482060980

Library of Congress Control Number: 2013902025

You can be the next Door-to-Door Millionaire by working directly with Lenny Gray!

His company, Rove Pest Control, is always looking to hire and partner with door-to-door sales reps and managers.

For more information, email Lenny at:
lennyg@d2dmillionaire.com

Visit his website at:
lennygray.com

"No one knows door-to-door sales like Lenny. His ability to train others to sell is uncanny. His communication skills are second to none."

McKay Bodily – VP/CFO,
Rove Pest Control, Inc. (Minnesota)

"I worked with Lenny Gray for nearly a decade and the lessons I learned from him transcend door-to-door sales. Because of his mentorship in sales, I am a more effective communicator and a more persuasive advocate."

Juan Godinez – Attorney-at-Law (Japan)

"I never thought Lenny training me as a door-to-door salesman would help me in my profession of building homes. Turns out reading body language and asking the right kinds of questions can help anyone in any industry."

Michael Jarman – Co-owner,
Rainier Custom Homes (Washington)

"Door-to-door sales taught me how to build relationships and solve issues within minutes of meeting someone. The lessons I learned from Lenny continue to help me every day, within and outside the office."

Kristi Brewer (CPA) – Senior Associate-Tax,
PwC (California)

"Lenny is a legend in the door-to-door sales industry. I have personally been trained by Lenny and his sales tactics will, without a doubt, increase your sales and make you a better sales rep."

Tom Karren – Partner, Vantage Marketing (Utah)

"Lenny's sales training not only led me to success on his door-to-door sales team, but I have been able to use his advice, strategy, and tactics to build my own successful digital marketing agency."

Mike Ramsey – Founder/President,
NiftyMarketing.com (Idaho)

"I practice law and run political campaigns and Lenny's training on speaking with new people is both the foundation of all of my courtroom presentations and also the base of what I teach campaign volunteers about direct voter contacting."

Josh Findley – Attorney-at-Law (Georgia)

"Lenny's training helped me to understand that being myself and helping others solve their problems would lead to success. Door-to-door work is difficult but very rewarding and I have used the lessons I learned with my young family. Problem solving and long days are a constant with growing toddlers!"

Hillary Handy – Mother-of-Three (Idaho)

"The sales training I received from Lenny has helped me in countless social situations outside of door-to-door sales. I feel that in my encounters with people, especially people I haven't met before, I have greater confidence and an increased ability to have meaningful conversation."

Dallin Bastian – College Student (Utah)

"Lenny can relate to anybody…he taught me how to be genuine and not salesy. The skillsets I gained from him have carried forward to my profession in public accounting."

Chris Siddoway – Audit Manager,
Deloitte (California)

"Lenny taught me more about overcoming people's concerns in a few short months of selling door to door than I ever learned through years of business and law school."

Brandon Ritchie – Attorney-at-Law (Idaho)

Contents

Preface

Ice to Eskimos

Wendy P. was the kindest, most pleasant, and possibly most popular girl in school. Although our families lived nearby and we attended the same church, we weren't always friends. You've probably heard the saying that a talented salesperson could "sell ice to Eskimos." Well, Wendy is Eskimo, and my best friend once told me that she was so far out of my league, I would have to be the best salesman ever to convince her to be my friend. He said that selling Wendy on my friendship would be as impressive as selling ice to Eskimos.

After selling pest control for three consecutive summers, Orkin Pest Control's primary marketing firm hired me to knock doors in several cities across the nation to determine whether these markets would be profitable locations for door-to-door sales teams.

On one occasion they sent me to Boise, Idaho—yes, Boise, Idaho—to sell annual pest control contracts. I didn't have high hopes for the market after the first person whose door I knocked said, "You're trying to sell me pest control? This has to be a joke. Why would I need a pest control service in Idaho?"

Despite this person's attitude, I ended up selling a lot of accounts that week I spent in Boise. In fact, it was during this trip I realized that I wasn't just a good salesman…I was a great salesman.

I was there in September, and after enduring a hot and humid summer in the South, I was thoroughly enjoying Idaho's cool fall evenings. One evening a man who had agreed to sign up for service invited me into his home. As I gathered his information and filled out the service agreement, he interrupted me and asked, "How much do you get paid for each sale you make?"

To which I responded with my typical comeback: "Not enough!"

This answer didn't satisfy him. He pressed. "No. Really. How much do you make when you sell a contract?"

Knowing he wasn't going away easy, I reluctantly told him, "I make around one hundred dollars in commissions for each contract."

He then asked, "What if I offered you a job that would pay at least three times as much as you're making now?"

Knowing I was making great money, I couldn't imagine making three times as much. He certainly had my attention, so I asked, "What exactly are you offering?"

He said, "I'm in the business of Internet advertising. I sell advertisements for websites."

Keep in mind this experience took place in the early 2000s, when Internet advertising was just starting to gain momentum as a viable advertising option.

He continued, "You could easily make around eighty thousand dollars a year!"

As much as I appreciated the man's offer, I realized he had no idea what kind of money I was making selling pest control contracts. I politely refused and continued to fill out his service agreement.

My willingness to brush off his proposal had irritated him, and he proclaimed, "You would have to be crazy to pass up on an offer like this."

I thanked him again for his offer but told him I was making good money and enjoyed what I was doing.

Not satisfied with my response, he asked, "How much did you make last month selling pest control?"

I really didn't want to tell him the truth. I didn't want to hurt his feelings or offend him in any way. After all, he was signing up for service, and I would be making commissions off of him! But I figured the only way to temper his persistence was to be completely honest with him, so I told him, "Last month, I made over twenty-five thousand dollars."

Looking a bit stunned, like I had just spoken to him in a foreign language, the man seemed to be waiting for me to smile or hint that I was pulling his leg…but I was dead serious.

He looked to the ground and muffled under his breath, "No way in hell this guy made that much last month…" Then he signed the pest control agreement and sent me on my way.

As I was walking away from his house, I came to the realization that I was a great salesman. I had a gift for sales and was making a remarkable living doing so. From that point on, I believed that, no matter where I was knocking, I could sell anything door to door.

If only Wendy could see me now. I was selling pest control to Idahoans…which was almost as impressive as selling ice to Eskimos.

Lester Hayes

I am done knocking doors. I've been successfully selling door to door since 1998, and I've sold millions of dollars in revenue of various products and services, but I made myself a promise that I would not knock another door for myself once I turned thirty-seven years old. Why thirty-seven? Well, that was my favorite professional football player's number—Lester Hayes, the greatest shutdown cornerback in the history of the NFL.

I began admiring the cornerback position as a fourth grader. In my first practice as a Little League football player, my coach identified me as a starting cornerback, though it happened inadvertently. Our quarterback was being taught how to throw a slant pass. As he reared back to throw the ball, I jumped the route by running in front of the receiver and knocked the ball down before it reached his hands. Somewhat surprised, my coach pointed at me and said, "There's our starting cornerback!"

At that point, whenever I watched a football game, I paid close attention to the cornerback position. And, having watched Lester Hayes on a few occasions, I could tell that he was the best of the bunch. Before the snap of the ball, he would crouch down low and position himself directly in front of the receiver he was guarding. His bump-and-run coverage was second to none, and he seemed to always know where the ball was going to be thrown.

When he retired from the game, he had been a two-time Super Bowl champion, Defensive Player of the Year, five-time Pro Bowler, and the self-proclaimed "only true Jedi" in the NFL...and, in my opinion, one of the best cornerbacks to ever play the game.

I believe I am one of the best door-to-door salesmen to ever knock doors. Although I've met a lot of great ones, none of them have accomplished what I've accomplished. I've proven my expertise through achievements of my own and through the successes of the hundreds of sales reps I've personally trained.

My sales techniques have not only been proven to work in a door-to-door setting but in many other sales environments as well. Think about it: door-to-door sales have to be the armpit of all sales opportunities. You are knocking on the doors of potential customers who may have never thought about purchasing the product or service you are peddling. For a sales job, it doesn't get any more difficult than that.

If you've succeeded as a door-to-door sales rep, any other sales situation should seem simple. Suppose you work as a salesperson at a jewelry store. When somebody walks into your store, they already have some level of interest in buying jewelry. They can be considered a warm lead. The salesperson didn't have to do anything to get them interested in purchasing jewelry. Whereas door-to-door sales reps rarely encounter warm leads but instead cold call on potential clients, which requires them to quickly build value in their product or service. For a door-to-door sales rep, the idea of approaching warm leads all day would seem like a dream come true.

Regardless of whether you are a salesperson who comfortably sits in a retail store waiting for warm leads or if you are cold calling out on the doors, this book teaches skills that turn ordinary sales reps into outstanding sales machines. My techniques will help you to attain your highest level of salesmanship.

The principles taught in this book will absolutely increase sales production. Having trained hundreds of door-to-door sales reps, I've seen it all—at least twice—

and it hasn't mattered if the sales rep is tall or short, fat or skinny, male or female, bald or blessed with a full head of hair; it doesn't matter what is sold, what state it's being sold in, or what tax bracket the customer is in. If used properly these principles generate sales at the highest level.

If you remember, Lester Hayes deemed himself as the "only true Jedi" of the NFL. But I have no desire to be the only true Jedi of sales. I want to pass on what I've learned so that you can become a Sales Jedi.

A little-known fact about Lester Hayes is that he was a lifelong stutterer until well into his professional career. He tended to stay quiet, rather than draw attention to his condition. For this reason, he was often looked at as not being very smart. But after successful treatment, people "couldn't shut him up," according to his former coach John Madden. It was then revealed that Lester was an articulate and intelligent man.

Over the years, I've never looked to draw attention to my success as a door-to-door salesman. But now that I'm officially retired from knocking doors, the time is right to reveal all of my secrets. I feel a sense of responsibility to pass on my wisdom to the thousands of sales reps who are in the stores and on the doors. I want to share the principles and techniques that will help you to become the next Sales Jedi.

Introduction

Door-to-door sales reps generate hundreds of millions of dollars annually for a variety of industries. Home security, home automation, pest control, yard maintenance, home television services, solar energy solutions and an assortment of home improvement products and services account for most of this revenue. Before the twenty-first century, door-to-door salespeople were primarily middle-aged suit-and-tie-clad businessmen carrying briefcases filled with cleaning products and encyclopedias. But now the industry is dominated by twenty-something's wearing polo shirts and cargo shorts and armed with PDAs broadcasting images and videos of their products and services in action.

Despite a general skepticism for door-to-door salespeople, several industries thrive marketing their products and services door to door. Highly successful companies are growing rapidly from their door-to-door efforts, and they continue to shape their business models around this type of marketing. Not only is business booming for companies marketing door to door, but the sales reps of these companies are cashing in as well.

College students knocking doors during summer break are averaging $25,000 in earnings in some industries, and full-time door-to-door sales reps are earning over $100,000 annually, making it no wonder that this line of work is becoming increasingly popular.

Colleges and universities are recognizing the importance of teaching sales skills to assist students in job placement after graduation. In 2007, forty-four US schools offered courses in sales—a number that jumped to 101 schools in 2011. Even MBA programs are getting into the game. In 2011, fifteen of them included sales courses as part of their graduate programs, and six offer an MBA with sales concentration. Business schools are investing in new sales programs, including door-to-door sales, to ensure their students get a strong return on investment from college. In fact, according to the 2011 Sales Education Foundation survey, about 90 percent of sales graduates have secured a job by graduation.

Door-to-door sales is also trending on the Internet. Search "door to door sales" on Google, and you'll find nearly 50 million related links on the topic. And on YouTube you'll find over 25,000 videos of self-proclaimed "experts" sharing advice and techniques of how they made it big as door-to-door salespeople.

Having had a long and successful career as a door-to-door salesman, I've tasted the success that can come with the profession. I've made millions of dollars from my own personal sales as well as the sales generated from the door-to-door sales teams I've trained for my own companies. Door-to-door sales is a legitimate way to make a lot of money in a short amount of time.

However, there are those who believe door-to-door salespeople are just fast-talking, fork-tongued scam artists selling nothing more than snake oil. Customers demand their money back and claim they were ballyhooed and bullied into buying a product or service that the sales rep falsely represented or strong-armed them into purchasing. I have witnessed, on occasion, sales reps using tactics of dishonesty and force to take advantage of potential customers. But these are a select few who unfortunately tarnish the reputation of the majority of door-to-door sales reps, who are upstanding and really good at sales.

Because of the dishonesty associated with the door-to-door sales industry, even I was reluctant to the idea of knocking doors. In 1997, a high school friend approached me trying to recruit me to knock doors for a pest control company in Albuquerque, New Mexico. As much as I trusted my friend, I'd heard the horror stories of door-to-door sales reps having to lie their way into making money, and that didn't resonate with my code of ethics. Besides, I was planning on getting married in a few months and had a good job working at a warehouse for $6.50 an hour.

Thankfully, my friend didn't give up on me. Six months later he called to inform me that he had earned over $20,000 and accepted a sales manager position for the following year. He wanted me to work in his office, to which I agreed because of his testament that the money-making opportunity in door-to-door sales was "legit." The following summer my wife and I packed almost everything we owned into our Nissan Altima and drove across the country to Birmingham, Alabama, so that I could sell pest control contracts door to door.

After four months in Birmingham, I had earned over $50,000 and was the top rookie sales rep for the nation's largest marketing company of door-to-door sales reps.

Game on!

While finishing my bachelor's degree, I sold door to door for two more summers, increasing my earnings by nearly $20,000 each summer. I was earning almost six figures in four months! I had paid for my college education with money to spare.

After graduating with my degree in Communications (broadcasting emphasis), I was offered a television reporter position at a local news station in Pasco, Washington. My proposed salary was $30,000, and the job description required me to work weekends and holidays. The news director told me that after three years as a reporter, I could possibly be considered for a news anchor position, earning $50,000 a year.

Thanks, but no thanks. I was making that kind of money as a door-to-door sales rep in just two months!

Needless to say, I passed on the offer to be on television and instead accepted a full-time position with the marketing company I had worked for as a door-to-door sales rep. During my two years with this marketing company, I developed a comprehensive sales training program that included a training manual and a series of training videos. I observed and trained hundreds of sales reps on the doors and was sent to test-market numerous cities across the nation to determine whether they were viable for door-to-door sales teams. And, as time permitted, I was able to knock doors and sell for myself.

The money was great, but the travel was grueling. After my wife and I had our firstborn, I realized the only way I could spend more time with family and less time traveling was to start a business of my own. I partnered with a colleague, McKay B., who had experience as a branch manager and was an expert in managing customers and running the day-to-day operations of a business. We made the perfect team.

In just five years, we became the largest residential pest control company in the state of Utah. We were able to accomplish this feat for many reasons, but at the top of the list was my ability to train our door-to-door sales reps to sell large volumes of accounts in a short amount of time. My training methods "worked like magic," according to one of our sales reps.

In 2007 one of the world's largest companies in our industry approached us with an offer to acquire our business. And, after much thought and discussion, we agreed on a multimillion-dollar acquisition—but we didn't stop there. We continued to build businesses with door-to-door sales teams across the nation that produced millions of dollars in revenue annually.

I firmly believe that successful sales reps are made, not born and that using truthful sales techniques are at the foundation of operating a successful business. The methods I've used and have trained others to use are proven to generate sales without compromising integrity. These techniques have been working effectively since the late '90s and will continue to do so if used correctly.

I have taught my sales techniques and methods to a multitude of audiences. With thousands of accounts sold for various industries, I have used my successes to personally provide on-the-door training to hundreds of sales reps, many of whom have continued on to become very successful in their careers as accountants, attorneys, engineers, physicians, teachers, business owners, and sales professionals. This book contains proven sales methods that work in the harshest sales environments and can benefit readers in any industry.

Chapter 1

Black Friday

The Friday following Thanksgiving is one of the busiest shopping days of the year. Commonly known as Black Friday, this is the day when many retailers start realizing profits and go from being in the red to the black.

In 2011, retail sales on Black Friday climbed 6.6 percent to an estimated $11.4 billion...in one day! In fact, total spending over Black Friday weekend in the same year reached a record $52.4 billion according to a survey by the National Retail Federation, which was up 16 percent from the previous year.

And according to the market research firm comScore, on Black Friday in 2012, for the first time in history, online retail e-commerce spending topped $1 billion.

On Thanksgiving Day, before their turkey is digested and the football games kick off, bargain-thirsty shoppers begin forming lines outside store entrances, with some retailers even opening their doors on Thanksgiving to capture more of the rabid consumers. Quickly the spirit of thanks and appreciation is replaced by threats and altercation.

In 2012, a police report was filed in California against a woman who doused her fellow shoppers with pepper spray in a bid to snag a discounted video game console.

In New York, a thirty-four-year-old Wal-Mart employee was trampled to death after an out-of-control mob of frenzied shoppers smashed through the front doors of the Long Island department store on Black Friday in 2008.

The insanity of Black Friday compelled one first-time shopper to exclaim, "I'll never forget what I saw. You see sides of people that they themselves didn't even know existed."

So, what is it that possesses these frenzied consumers to a state of madness and mayhem? Bottom line...they crave the acquisition of the limited supplies of merchandise that retailers offer for a limited time at a discounted price. These three components (**limited supply**, **limited time** and **discount**) create the perfect storm known as Black Friday and when bargain buyers get their hands on these elusive goods, they laud themselves as shopping archaeologists, who very well could have beaten Indian Jones to the Canyon of the Crescent Moon to discover the Holy Grail.

Black Friday is a perfect example of why I'm convinced human nature drives us to attaining the exclusive, winning and saving money. Thus, when communicating with potential customers, sales reps who are able to replicate the spirit of Black Friday will capitalize on the innate desires of mankind.

For this to occur, the following must be expressed. First, there has to be a discount offered that is limited to a certain number of people. This compels the potential customer into buying the product or service before somebody else does.

Second, there has to be a time line given for when the discount expires. The time line can be determined by supply or the time frame that the sales rep will be in the area.

If the potential customer believes they can buy a product or service anytime they want to at the same price that is being offered, they will purchase the item on their terms, not the sales rep's. Therefore, a line in the sand must be drawn as to the amount of products or services being offered at a discount and the length of time until the discount expires.

As a rookie sales rep in Omaha, Nebraska, David A. had his best day selling on his last day knocking doors. I called and asked him what he did differently this day than what he had been doing the other one hundred-plus days he'd been working, and this is what he told me:

"I knew this would be my last day selling here... probably forever. So, I emphasized how important it was for people to know that the discount I was offering was for today and today only. If somebody told me they wanted to think about it and call me back tomorrow, I told them I wouldn't be in the area and if they wanted the discount I had to know today."

David gave a specific time line for when his discount would expire and wasn't willing to budge even one day. It was literally now or never for him to make the sale. His willingness to stick to his time line paid off in a big way, as he earned nearly $800 on his last day on the doors.

Once you've identified a time line, you must stay true to it—even if it means walking away from a potential sale. In the end, sales reps make far more sales sticking to a time line than they'll miss out on by giving the potential customer the time they request to make their decision. Prospective customers are notorious for telling sales reps they will call them back once they've had a chance to think about their offer. But, in my experience, this turns out to be an empty promise in most cases.

When a potential customer asks for more time to consider an offer, you might counter by saying, "You can think about it as long as you'd like, but because I only have two more reservations that I can offer at a discount, I have to give them to the first two people who commit. If somebody gets them before you have a chance to decide, I'm sure you understand that the offer is first-come, first-serve. I will continue talking to your neighbors. When I get down to my last available opening, I would be happy to stop back by so you have some time to think about it."

The person's response will give a good indication as to whether they really do need more time to make up their mind and are genuinely interested in taking advantage of the offer.

If they continue to indicate they need more time to think about it, you could respond, "Take your time and make sure you really want it. Once these last two spots are filled, the service will go back to full price. You can always call and pay full price but if you want to take advantage of the discount, I will need to know today because I'm sure somebody else will reserve the spots."

Sales reps should make sales on their terms, not their potential customer's. The desire of the potential customer to buy the product or service should supersede the sales rep's desire to sell it. Willingly walking away from a possible sale proves that the time line to take advantage of the discount is legitimate. Having confidence in the exclusivity and time line of the discount incites action from potential clients. And as sales reps portray this attitude, they are able to awaken the inner-Black Friday shoppers in their contacts and instill in them the desire to get the discount before somebody else.

Chapter 2

Make Them Want It

Isn't it interesting how important a possession becomes when somebody else wants it? I observe this regularly with my kids. If one of my sons starts playing with his brother's toy, even if it's a toy that hasn't been played with in months, it immediately becomes a prized possession. The only thing that matters to my son is that his brother gives up his toy so he can once again claim it.

Of course, five minutes after he gets it back, the toy is once again disregarded. But the moment the toy has value to somebody else, despite it being buried in a heap of other toys, its importance becomes immeasurable.

These childhood instincts remain with us in adulthood. Remember the last time a neighbor asked to borrow something from your garage and didn't return it when they said they would? Soon enough you start missing that item as if it's the most important thing in your garage. You need it, you think of ways you can use it, and the fact that somebody else has it drives you insane!

I once sold a car to a man who never saw the vehicle in person. He initially stated that he would need to take the car for a test drive and have his auto mechanic look it over. However, when another potential buyer came into the running to purchase the car, he decided the online pictures of the car were sufficient. He agreed to buy the vehicle and immediately wired the money into my bank account before the other potential buyer had a chance to counter.

I believe that human nature makes us desire that which others deem to have value. To be a successful door-to-door sales rep, you have to make your potential clients want what you are offering. You can accomplish this by letting your contacts know that their neighbors have purchased what you are selling at a discounted rate, and they have the opportunity to do the same. And, if they pass up your offer, they will miss out on the discount because somebody else will take advantage of it.

This technique only works if you know the names of your potential customer's neighbors. Using the names of current customers or others you have spoken to, which is commonly referred to as *name-dropping*, helps you to establish credibility with your contacts. Then you can start the process of making them want what their neighbors already have. To be successful in sales, you must develop the habit of *name-dropping* with every contact. The most effective *name-dropping* techniques are:

1. Asking for names of contacts who reject your offer
2. Using names of your company's current customers
3. Using names of customers whom you have sold

Asking for Names

If you are selling in an area without customers, it's best to start asking for names of everybody you contact. As you gather and use the names of those who reject your offer, you are still giving yourself a reason to be in that area.

When potential clients reject your offer, you might say, "I appreciate your time. Maybe you'll be interested some other time. Again, my name is Millie." And while reaching your hand out to shake the person's hand, you might ask, "And what was your name?"

Then, as you come in contact with that person's neighbors, you could begin your conversation by saying, "Hello. My name is Millie, and I'm with Four Leaf Clover Lawn Care. I was just talking to Cindy next door and wanted to let you know…"

This method for collecting and using names allows you to do so without compromising your integrity. You are not saying the person you spoke with is a customer. On the contrary, you are just letting that person know that you have spoken to their neighbor.

However, if your contact asks if the neighbors whose names you dropped are customers, you would of course explain that they are not. You could even expound as to why they chose not to accept your offer.

Current Customers

Depending on the products or services you are offering and the company you work for, privacy issues may prevent you from obtaining current customer data. However, if you have been granted permission to use the names of current customers, you will certainly want to do so.

Once your contacts realize their peers have been using your products or services, they are much more likely to consider purchasing these items from you. Few people want to be the guinea pig of the neighborhood by buying something that nobody else has shown interest in purchasing.

To use current customer names, you could begin a conversation with a prospective customer by saying, "I'm not sure if you are aware, but the Sorensen family next door and the Larson family down the street are customers of ours, and we're offering a couple of their neighbors the opportunity to get our services at a discounted rate…"

This approach gives you a valid purpose for being in the neighborhood and asking others for their business.

You already have customers on the street, so of course it makes sense for you to get more business in an area where you have an existing customer base.

Using Your Customers' Names

Finally, it's absolutely critical that you use the names of the clients you have sold. In fact, if you have a signed service agreement in hand, you should begin your approach by showing the potential customer their neighbor's information on the agreement and explaining, "I was just finishing up with Jack and Bonnie across the street (pointing to their house), and we are delivering our products to their home tomorrow. And being that our delivery truck will be in the neighborhood, I can offer a couple of their neighbors an incredible discount on our products…"

A signed contract gives you the most legitimate reason to ask your customer's neighbors if they have an interest in your product or service. Even if a house is adorned with "No Soliciting" signs and a barbed-wire fence, you can confidently approach the home knowing that you have their neighbor's signed contract in hand and thus the most justifiable reason for letting them know what their neighbors are doing.

Under very few circumstances would you approach a potential customer without using names of people who live in the area. Forgetting to name-drop will send up red flags to your contacts and make you appear as an uninvited guest in their neighborhood. By getting in the habit of properly *name-dropping*, you will put your contacts at ease because they know you know who they know...you know?

Now that you have names to drop, you can begin the process of making your contacts want what you've got. This is effectively accomplished by enticing them to buy what their neighbors already have or by giving them the opportunity to buy something at a discount before their neighbors beat them to it.

You will increase your sales production if you can either convince your contacts to join their neighbors in purchasing your products or services—also known as the *bandwagon effect*—or invoke the spirit of competition amongst neighbors to entice them to get the deal before somebody else does.

The *bandwagon effect* often occurs in politics when the media or persons of influence give an endorsement to a particular candidate or issue. Some voters base their decisions on whom and what to vote for solely on how others are voting, rather than researching the candidates and examining the issues on their own.

In an attempt to capitalize on the *bandwagon effect*, US presidential candidates spend a lot of their time campaigning in Iowa. This is because the Iowa caucuses are the first major electoral event of the nominating process. Although only about 1 percent of the nation's delegates are chosen by the Iowa State Convention, the caucuses serve as an early indicator of which candidates for president might win the nomination of their political party.

Senator George McGovern, the Democratic contender in the 1972 election, explained the significance of Iowa like this: "Iowa is terribly important. It's the first test in the nation, where we get any test at all."

Another way to call people to action is to invoke in them the spirit of competition. As human beings we are naturally motivated by challenges, whereas we tend to lose interest in that which is simple and uncomplicated.

Take, for instance, the dating scene. Playing hard to get can make a person more desirable to his or her suitors. Elusiveness rouses the thrill of the chase. On the contrary, interest can be lost quickly in those who always make themselves readily available. Where there is no challenge, there will ultimately be no interest.

Sales reps who are able to influence others to do what their neighbors are doing and plant the seeds of competition within their contacts will start the process of generating more interest from their potential customers—which, in turn, generates more sales.

The concept of "How to Make Them Want It" can be summarized as follows: Begin by properly *name-dropping* to establish your credibility. Then either use the *bandwagon effect* or incite competition amongst neighbors by your offer. As you use these techniques, your contacts will view you less as a stranger peddling unwanted goods and more as a messenger communicating valuable information.

And that is the *Secret Sauce of Success* in door-to-door sales. You are a door-to-door salesperson, but you can't be perceived as one. Your potential clients should simply think of you as a messenger of information. And if you can accomplish that, success is certain.

Chapter 3

Secret Sauce of Success

In the fifteenth and sixteenth centuries, when a messenger delivered news that the receiving party was opposed to, the innocent messenger would frequently be tortured or put to death.

Shakespeare expressed the saying "Don't shoot the messenger" in his plays *Henry IV, Part 2* (1598) and *Antony and Cleopatra* (1623).

When a messenger tells Cleopatra that Antony has married another, she threatens to treat the messenger's eyes as balls. Prior to that, Sophocles expressed a related sentiment in Antigone: "No one loves the messenger who brings bad news."

On the contrary, messengers bringing good news are celebrated, but unfortunately door-to-door sales reps are stereotyped as being messengers of bad news. Thus, being identified as a messenger of good news, instead of a door-to-door salesperson increases the probability of being received favorably. In my experience as a door-to-door salesman, I've received the praises of many customers:

"You're such a great salesman!"

"You really talked us into it."

"I just can't say no to you."

Although great to hear, none of these compliments can compare to the compliment of all compliments, the *ultimate compliment* for door-to-door sales reps:

"I'm sure glad you weren't one of those door-to-door salespeople."

When a customer expresses this sentiment, the sales rep should be commended for comprehending the *Secret Sauce of Success*. Once customers don't recognize you as a door-to-door salesperson, you have officially become a professional door-to-door salesperson. Strive to receive the *ultimate compliment*.

Acting like a salesperson is a sure way to lose sales. If you live up to the preconceived expectations of a salesperson, your contacts will have you right where they want you: five feet in the ground, with only one more foot to go. These expectations have developed over time. As sales reps have inundated potential customers' doorsteps over the years, homeowners have formed their own attitudes of how to deal with these uninvited visitors.

Effective sales reps don't live up to the beliefs; they strive to be unique, likeable, informed, and willing to walk away from potential sales to prove they are not a cliché salesperson. They make every effort to make an un-expected impression and receive the *ultimate compliment.*

Remember, you are simply a messenger of good news.

The following are suggestions for how to transform from a stereotypical salesperson into a model messenger:

- Be a Seven
- Be Likeable
- Be Informed
- Be Willing to Walk Away

Be a Seven

If you're honest with yourself, you're probably a boring person. In your everyday routine, you are most likely as dull as dishwater. I know I am. Even in a group setting, I'd rather stay quiet and observe than draw attention to myself.

I'm an only child. We're a strange breed. We don't need approval or attention from others because we've had to learn how to entertain ourselves without an audience.

But in sales, your boring old self won't cut it. A change must take place. You have to be capable of adopting a different persona, as if you're an actor in a movie. And if you don't accept this role, you will likely bore your contacts with the everyday you.

Consider the volume level on a television. With the setting at a one, you might barely hear anything. Conversely, when cranked to a ten, your eardrums are overloaded with sound. How sales reps communicate is similar to the volume level of a television.

In my experience, most sales reps are preprogrammed at a four or five: plain old ordinary. There is nothing unique or entertaining about them, and within seconds of opening their mouths, their contacts completely tune them out. You cannot be common to be successful as a sales rep. Ordinary door-to-door sales reps get cast off doorsteps into the heap of unsuccessful sales reps of the past.

It might be acceptable to talk to an acquaintance at a four or five level, but, as you are meeting potential clients, this level just doesn't cut it. Remember: you are an actor, and the doorstep is your stage. You must shed the cocoon of your ordinary self and metamorphose into somebody so captivating and interesting that your every word is followed.

I believe the perfect volume level is a seven. Being a seven isn't ordinary, but it's also not so over the top that your potential contact's "fight or flight" instincts kick in. Sevens are able to keep their contact's attention longer because they are entertaining and talk at a level where it is easy to be heard.

It's important to stay true to who you are but to also understand that the regular old you will likely drive your contacts down the path of being uninterested and uninspired. As a sales rep you are an entertainer and must do the entertaining.

You will notice an immediate difference in how you are received by potential customers as you turn up your volume a few notches.

Be Likeable

In door-to-door sales you already have two strikes against you. First, you are an uninvited guest. Second, you have arrived offering goods and services that have not been requested. Therefore, you have to give potential customers a reason to like you, or you'll be striking out quicker than the guy at a pool party with the hairy back.

There is truth to the old sales adage that you are selling yourself just as much as you are selling your product. In fact, Juan G., one of the most successful sales reps I've ever trained, told me he would have several customers tell him the reason they signed up for service wasn't because of the service itself or the discount he was offering, but they mostly bought the service because they liked him. Everything else was just icing on the cake.

Likeability can be achieved by finding ways to compliment your contacts. It's simple really. As a messenger you don't need to begin your conversation with your sales pitch. You should start by giving your contact a compliment about something you observe in their yard or home, or even give them a compliment about something they are wearing.

After you've given a compliment, then ask a follow-up question. A simple yet effective example of this could be: "I cannot believe how green your grass is. How do you keep it so green?"

A comment and question as effortless as this can get your contact liking you right off the bat. You have already set yourself apart from all the other door-to-door sales reps who cut right to the chase of their sales pitches. It's much easier to like somebody who is complimentary.

The following are remarks that I've used to help put potential customers at ease and get on their good side.

When a dog precedes the homeowner to the door, no matter what the size of the dog, I say with a smile:

"I see you have your attack dog here. What kind of dog is it?"

Most people love their pets. Therefore, asking questions about a pet is a surefire way to make you more likeable.

If somebody is in their driveway washing a car, you might exclaim:

"I hear this is where the free car wash is. Can I pull up my car next?"

And one of my personal favorites is when somebody is out doing yard work and you say:

"Let me finish taking care of your yard work, and I'll let you finish my job for me. What does your spouse pay you by the hour to do yard work?"

To become likeable, you have to treat your contacts like friends, so don't hesitate to bring humor into the conversation if the opportunity presents itself.

Albert A., a new sales rep in Nashville, Tennessee, told me he was having difficulty coming up with ways to put his potential clients at ease. As I observed him in conversation, I concurred. He began every conversation the same and came across as a stereotypical salesman.

As we talked about his shortcoming, he challenged me to find something creative to say at the next door we knocked on. I could tell him what I would say, and he would relay it to the potential customer.

As we walked up the driveway of the next house, the garage door was open and we saw several diaper boxes stacked up in the garage that appeared to be used for storing clothing.

Albert looked at me with a big smile and said, "How do you suppose you'll relate to this?"

I thought about it for a few seconds, and after I knocked on the front door, I told him what he should say. The customer answered the door, and Albert proceeded:

"We noticed all of the diaper boxes in your garage and wanted to add to your collection. Do you prefer Huggies or Pampers?"

It worked! The customer bellowed out a laugh and proceeded to explain why he had the boxes in his garage. The barrier of a salesman had been torn down, a friendly conversation ensued, and Albert learned a valuable lesson in the effectiveness of finding unique ways to relate to contacts and getting them to like you.

Be Informed

The following summer in Nashville, I was on the doors training Dallin B. and we came across a man wearing a West Virginia Mountaineers sweatshirt. This was kind of an odd thing to see in the Volunteer state, so I made a quick comment to the potential customer about a coach at WVU whom I remembered hearing about on the radio. My comment had very little depth, but this minuscule amount of information completely put the man at ease and he opened up to us like we were his old college buddies.

Because I was informed about something that was important to him, the barriers of a door-to-door salesperson were bulldozed. I have found that sales reps who are informed on a broad spectrum of topics are far more capable of coming across as messengers rather than sales reps.

In Omaha, Nebraska, I sold a husband and wife while training Ben W. As we walked away from the home after finishing up the paperwork, Ben turned to me and said, "I had no idea you knew so much about soccer."

To which I replied, "I really don't know that much about soccer, but I guess I knew enough to make it seem as though I was a big fan."

By being informed and observant, you'll be surprised how easy it is to find ways to relate to your contacts. And as you do, they'll be more relaxed because you'll be talking about things they appreciate. If you notice a team flag in their yard, fishing equipment in their garage, a piano in their home, or a unique piece of art displayed, make a comment about it. You'll be surprised how much more willing people will be to talk to you.

By the way, referring back to the guy wearing the West Virginia sweatshirt, in case you were wondering, yes, we made the sale—and I specifically credit it to knowing a little something about a topic he cared about.

Be Willing to Walk Away

Finally, you have to be willing to walk away from potential sales to make the point that you are simply delivering a message and are not a stereotypical salesperson. This is not an easy thing to do, but there will be instances when you will want to excuse yourself from a conversation and let your contact know you will be taking your offer elsewhere.

The following are the three most common occurrences when you should walk away from a potential sale:

First, be willing to walk away when your contact doesn't accept the terms of your offer. If you offer a discount with a time line and the customer tries extending that time line, you could say, "You can call the office another time and pay full price, but I only have a dozen more products I can sell for the discount, and your neighbors will probably buy them up quickly."

Second, be willing to walk away when your contact tells you they will call you when they are ready to make a purchase. Similarly, to the previous example, you might say, "As I've mentioned, I only have a couple more openings on the schedule that I can offer at a discount. It is a great deal, so I know one of your neighbors will take it, but you are welcome to call me at another time and pay full price."

Finally, be willing to walk away when your contact stops asking questions, keeps looking at their watch, or appears uncomfortable with your being there. You could say, "I'm in a bit of hurry to get appointments made for the installation of these last two systems that I'm discounting. I'll tell you what, feel free to call the office at your convenience for the normal pricing, but I'll go talk with your neighbors to get these discounted appoint-ments scheduled."

In order to maximize your opportunity for making sales, you must be willing to walk away from contacts that are not progressing. It makes no sense to waste your time with them while other potential sales may be much more likely to receive your offer.

Being willing to walk away from potential sales will sometimes create unexpected results. While knocking doors in Verdigris, Oklahoma, I had nearly sold a house-wife but wanted her to verify with her husband before letting her sign up for the service. She told me her hus-band didn't like being bothered at work and that she would have to talk to him later that evening. So, I told her, "That's fine. I may not have any more discounted spots on the schedule if your neighbors take them, but if that's the case I can still get you scheduled for service at the regular price once your husband approves."

She was visibly bothered by the idea of missing out on the discount, but I wasn't about to sign her up with-out her husband's approval. During my first couple of years selling door to door, I probably broke up a mar-riage or two and got in the middle of several spousal arguments, so my days of signing up one spouse without the other knowing about it were over.

Nonetheless, in this instance, she wouldn't commit to calling her husband, so I excused myself and continued down the street.

Not more than five minutes later, this same lady came running down the street in my direction yelling, "Lenny, wait! Lenny!" Once she reached me, winded and out of breath, she managed to ask, "Do you still have one of those discounted spots open for tomorrow?"

Despite her reluctance to call her husband at work, the thought of her neighbors taking those discounted spots gave her enough motivation to make the call and get his consent.

This experience was rare, but proves the point that as a messenger, and not a salesperson, you have to be willing to walk away from potential sales. Make sales on your terms, and if the potential client isn't willing to accept these terms, somebody else will. This attitude will help you to effectively gauge your contact's interest as they demonstrate their willingness to make the necessary arrangements to take advantage of your offer.

Chapter 4

Pied Piper

Successful people, although praised by many, also receive their share of criticism. Bill Gates cofounded the world's largest personal-computer software company, Microsoft. His ingenuity and product strategy in the industry made him one of the wealthiest human beings on the planet. His net worth is estimated at $65 billion. *Forbes* magazine ranked him as the fourth most powerful person in the world in 2012, and *Time* magazine named him as one of the one hundred people who most influenced the twentieth century.

Despite his achievements and acquired wealth, there are still those who question his capabilities. Steve Jobs, former cofounder, chairman, and CEO of Apple, Inc., was quoted in his biography as saying of Gates, "Bill is basically unimaginative and has never invented anything, which is why I think he's more comfortable now in philanthropy than technology. He just shamelessly ripped off other people's ideas" (Isaacson 2011, 173).

Paul Allen, cofounder of Microsoft, also took his shots at Gates. In Allen's book, *Idea Man: A Memoir by the Cofounder of Microsoft*, he was quoted as saying, "When I got mad, I stayed mad for weeks. I don't know if Bill noticed the strain on me, but everyone else did. Some said Bill's management style was a key ingredient in Microsoft's early success, but that made no sense to me. Why wouldn't it be more effective to have civil and rational discourse? Why did we need knock-down, drag-out fights?" (Allen 2011, 115).

During my first year selling door to door, other sales reps in the company were critical of my success. I was the leading rookie sales rep in the nation, and it seemed everybody had their opinion as to why this was the case. Some naysayers declared that I just happened to be talking to the right people at the right time, while others said the neighborhoods and cities I was assigned to work in were perfectly primed for sales.

Although my sales totals increased year after year, there were still those who doubted my abilities and made up excuses why I was able to sell so many accounts. No matter how many I sold or where I sold them, some could not be convinced that my expertise in communication and unmatched work ethic were primarily the reasons behind my improbable sales accomplishments.

The most ridiculous excuse I ever heard earned me a nickname in the pest control industry. A skeptical colleague once said the reason I was doing so well was because pests would follow me to the areas I was assigned to knock. Thus, I was dubbed *The Pied Piper of Pest Control*.

I can't say I've ever played a magical pipe and ushered rodents out of Hamelin (or any other town, for that matter), but I am convinced of my ability to lead people into buying what I'm selling. In fact, I believe if I parachuted out of a plane and landed in any city, I could sell a product or service door to door. Rural, suburban, urban—it wouldn't matter. Of course, some products are more likely to sell to certain demographics, but I believe most anything can be sold most anywhere.

Nevertheless, some sales reps make the argument that sales are only made because of luck. I will admit that there is a bit of luck involved in sales, especially door-to-door sales. Because door-to-door sales reps are purely cold calling, they do have to come across potential customers at the right time. There are many instances when sales reps knock on the doors of would-be customers who are unapproachable because they are out running errands, on the phone, out of town, or in the middle of dinner. So, in that sense, sure there is some luck in door-to-door sales, but once you have a potential customer engaged in conversation, luck goes out the window and it becomes a matter of having the skills to know what to say, how to say it, and when to say it that ultimately increases the probability of making the sale.

Consistency is the key to becoming a great sales rep, and consistent production is typically preceded by a consistent attitude. Sales reps should frequently remind themselves to maintain a demeanor of steadiness from day to day and even from door to door. It's counterproductive to get too elated after an effective day or to get too distressed after a difficult day. No matter if you've had your best day selling or ended up with a goose egg, when you wake up the next morning, you start with the same number of sales as everybody else: zero. And although it's important to keep momentum from successes and learn from mistakes, in sales, you only make money today from what you produce today.

The following pages will outline the components that will help you to achieve consistent production. But keep in mind that none of these suggestions involves playing a magic flute. Onward, Pied Piper!

Every Contact a Customer

It's easy to formulate an opinion about somebody before getting to know them. As human beings, we do it all the time. As sales reps, you can't do it or you'll never sell consistently.

There is no secret formula for determining what a customer looks like, acts like, or talks like. Customers come in all shapes and sizes. So, every time a door is opened, believe that the person standing in front of you will be your next customer.

An account was given of a young man who had been the most successful missionary in his area. His supervisor asked him why he had such phenomenal success when others didn't. The missionary said that he attempted to baptize every person he met.

He said that if he knocked on the door and saw a man smoking a cigar, dressed in old clothes, and seemingly uninterested in anything—particularly religion—the missionary would picture in his own mind what that man would look like under a different set of circumstances. In his mind he would look at him as clean-shaven and wearing a white shirt and white trousers. And the missionary could see himself leading that man into the waters of baptism.

Visualizing each person you come in contact with as a sale will help you avoid the mistake of prejudgment. I cringe when I hear sales reps declare they are incapable of selling certain groups of people. It might be older people, rich people, or even certain races of people they categorized as unsellable. There is danger in this type of thinking because limits are being placed on potential sales, and discrimination can ensue.

In 2005, Dave H. was one of the most promising new sales reps we had ever hired. In his first three days, he produced over $3,000 in sales. At that point he was not

LENNY GRAY

only outperforming all the other new sales reps, he had even outsold all of our experienced sales reps.

After two months he had generated over $23,000 in new business and was the top-producing rookie sales rep in the company. But as remarkable as his first two months were, his next two months were even more extraordinary—but not because of his production. It was his lack of production that was so unbelievable. Dave only sold $7,500 in new business during his remaining two months on the job.

In all of my years in door-to-door sales, I have never seen such an extreme fall-off in production from a sales rep. Typically the first two months are the most difficult for new sales reps because they are trying to figure out a new skill, and the learning curve initially slows their production. But after a while, the skill is learned and production increases.

But Dave's experience was the complete opposite. He started off strong and then completely unraveled. I had knocked doors with him on two occasions before his struggles, and there was no indication that he was communicating something that would cause such a drastic decline. As his production began slipping, I made it a point to knock doors with him for a third time so I could observe firsthand whether he was doing something contrary to what I had taught him.

58

It didn't take long for me to identify his problem. As we were walking up the driveway of the first three doors we approached, he would say, "This one's not a sale."

Although he was right, no sales were made at these three houses, I had never witnessed a sales rep who called his shot before knocking on a door. Honestly, it was kind of creepy. Dave had somehow turned into a summoner of sales, who was relying on premonition instead of proficiency.

Dave wasn't just prejudging his contacts, he was pre-prejudging them. He had determined that he could identify a sale before he even identified whom he was trying to sell. His thought process was clearly skewed, and the results were evident.

When a door opens, the person in front of you should have a clean slate. They have to be viewed as a potential sale from the get-go. Your best effort must be made to convince that person why they need to buy your product or service. You cannot afford to make unsubstantiated assumptions about anybody you come in contact with, or you will hamper your ability to make sales.

All Areas Produce

In 2008, an experienced team of sales reps in Minneapolis, Minnesota, was frustrated because of their lack of production. They weren't making sales at the level they had been accustomed to in other states, and they began pointing fingers at the areas they were assigned to knock.

As the days passed, their numbers continued to trail off, and these sales reps were convinced that Minnesota was to blame. They told their branch manager that the area wasn't conducive to selling his services, and there were no good areas to knock in the North Star State. They demanded to be transferred to another office.

Before giving in to their request, the branch manager made a request of his own. He asked an experienced sales rep who had been successfully selling in Nebraska to spend a week knocking doors in Minnesota to see if the sales team was justified in their assessment of the area.

Juan G. made arrangements to spend the week in Minnesota, and after two days he had already outsold the sales team's output for the week. In fact, Juan ended the week doubling the sales total of the entire team.

Thanks to Juan, these sales reps viewed their area in a new light. They realized the area wasn't to blame but rather their attitude toward the area. And with their excuses no longer validated, the sales team began generating sales at a level they were accustomed to.

Many sales reps fall prey to a concept referred to as *pigeon-holing*. This notion that a sales rep is only able to sell accounts in specific types of homes can ensnare even the most skilled salesperson.

In 2011, a sales team of ten was assigned to knock in Oklahoma City, Oklahoma, and its surrounding areas. After two and a half months, the sales reps were convinced they had knocked on every sellable door in the area and it was time for them to move on to another office.

For reference, OKC and its surrounding metro is populated by roughly 1.3 million people, and there are nearly 550,000 housing units in those areas.

Therefore, to knock every sellable door, each of the ten sales reps would have had to knock on approximately 820 doors a day for two and a half months. In an eight-hour working day, that's knocking on more than a hundred doors an hour! Not a likely feat, but certainly not impossible—that is, if you are just knocking on doors and not talking to anybody. Granted, not every home of the 550,000 would be approachable because of vacancy or construction, but to think that a team of ten sales reps could saturate a market the size of Oklahoma City in just over two months was absurd.

Unless of course they had *pigeon-holed* areas they were and weren't willing to knock. And, upon further investigation, that was exactly what was happening. This sales team had convinced one another that the only areas worth knocking were neighborhoods with homes under three years old and they would be wasting their time knocking on doors over three years old. This mind-set led them to believe that less than 10 percent of the approachable homes in the area were viable knocking options. Not to mention they didn't even consider double-knocking homes in the neighborhoods they did consider worthy of their time.

This shortsightedness nearly led to this sales team's demise. Fortunately, effective training in areas with homes over three years old was demonstrated, and the team spent the entire summer successfully knocking in and around Oklahoma City.

Sales reps need to understand that there are sales to be had in all types of neighborhoods and homes. Old, new, brick, stucco, big, small—it really doesn't matter, as long as the parameters determined by their employer are followed.

My first attempt at door-to-door sales was in 1998 in Birmingham, Alabama. My first assigned area was in the city of Homewood, located just south of Birmingham. At the time, this quaint city's population was under 25,000.

Initially my hope was to spend my entire four months knocking in Homewood, but I soon realized that I would run out of area in about a month. During my last days in Homewood, I worried myself sick that I would not be as productive once transferred to another city. And one evening, as the sun was setting, I had about thirty minutes of daylight remaining until I would end my day, so I decided to drive to a neighboring city to knock a few doors and hopefully end my speculation of whether I would have success outside of Homewood.

The city I chose was Mountain Brook. To give some context, this city had never been a favorite of door-to-door sales reps. In fact, most avoided working there altogether. It was commonly referred to as the "rich city" where sales were too difficult to come by because the people were too proud and unwilling to listen.

As I drove around looking for a neighborhood to knock, it became obvious that I wasn't in Homewood. I was accustomed to knocking on the doors of homes that were roughly 1,500 square feet, and the homes in Mountain Brook were at least double that size. As I got out of my car and approached the first house, which seemed like a mansion, I was trembling inside, having little to no confidence in my ability to sell outside of my comfort zone.

An older woman answered the door, and I gave her my best opening line. Soon afterward she brought her husband to the door so I could explain to him why I was there and what I was offering. She specifically told me that I must address her husband as "Doctor." She informed me that he had earned that title by his years of schooling and practice as a physician. I certainly hadn't heard that in Homewood.

After conversing for about ten minutes, the "Doctor" and his wife were ready to commit and sign on the dotted line. I sold an account in Mountain Brook, to a doctor, on the first door I knocked! My confidence was at an all-time high. From that time on, I became less concerned about where I was knocking and more concerned about my attitude toward my area. If I expected the area to be good, it likely would be.

The best sales reps produce consistently because they don't *pigeon-hole* themselves into believing that only certain neighborhoods produce sales. They are confident in their ability to make sales in whatever area they are assigned to work.

Next-Door Neighbors

Another technique that leads to selling accounts on more of a consistent basis is targeting next-door neighbors of current customers. There is a much higher probability of selling the immediate neighbors of current customers for two reasons in particular. First is the possibility that next-door neighbors have *similar needs,* and second is the concept of *keeping up with the Joneses.*

Similar Needs

There are two access points into my neighborhood, and each option requires the ascension of a steep hill to get to the street where my house is located. During the winter, when these streets start to accumulate snow, they are impossible to climb without all-season or snow tires.

I learned this the hard way my first winter living in the area, ruining a relatively new set of tires after slipping and sliding for nearly an hour in an attempt to ascend one of these hills after a snow storm. The next day after that experience, I purchased a set of snow tires...and so did a lot of my neighbors. Every car owner on the street had a need for tires that were capable of climbing in the snow, and the nearest tire store benefited greatly because of this necessity.

In 2002, I was assigned to test-market some suburbs of Chicago, Illinois, and determine whether the area would be favorable for door-to-door sales teams to sell a pest control service. For three days I knocked doors in Algonquin, about an hour northwest of Chicago.

One neighborhood I began knocking happened to be built around a large gravel pit. Fortunately for me, this gravel pit was home to hundreds, if not thousands, of mice. And during the late summer and early fall, as nighttime temperatures began cooling off, these mice would migrate to the houses next to the gravel pit in search of shelter from the cold.

Working in this neighborhood for just three days, I sold over $17,000 in new business (thirty-three accounts)! Because the homeowners shared a similar need, I almost effortlessly sold next-door neighbor after next-door neighbor. In fact, the only neighbors I didn't sign up were those who were already customers or had recently signed up for service with another company.

In Portland, Oregon, while training a couple of door-to-door sales reps selling home security systems, I learned the importance of contacting next-door neighbors of current customers.

We were assigned to knock doors in a neighborhood where a customer had recently had a security system installed because their home had been burglarized a few days earlier. As we arrived in the area, I suggested we initially try contacting the next-door neighbors of the current customer. One of the sales reps agreed, but the other decided to start knocking at the other end of the street.

A short time later, after selling both next-door neighbors of the current customer, we met up with the other sales rep who had yet to make any sales on the street. I then took him to the house next door to the neighbors we had just sold and signed those neighbors up too. In fact, later that day he ended up selling somebody who had previously turned him down only because their next-door neighbor had just signed up for installation. In total, the three of us ended up selling six houses in a row and eight of eleven houses on that street.

It's likely that next-door neighbors share similar needs. Therefore, contacting the next-door neighbors of current customers will make a huge impact on being able to sell accounts consistently.

Keeping up with the Joneses

This saying refers to the comparison of oneself to one's neighbor as a benchmark for or the accumulation of material goods. To fail to "keep up with the Joneses" is perceived as demonstrating socioeconomic or cultural inferiority.

In the neighborhood where I was raised, my family lived next door to the same people for eight years. I will refer to them as the Smith family. The Smiths were great neighbors, and our families spent a lot of time together. The only downside of this family was that Mr. Smith had a serious case of *keeping up with the Joneses* when it came to my family.

In just fourteen months, the following events took place at our house and the Smiths' house. In the summer we had a chain-link fence installed; shortly thereafter, Mr. Smith had the same company install the same chain-link fence around his yard. At the onset of winter, we bought a snow blower; within days of this purchase, Mr. Smith bought a snow blower. For Christmas, Santa Claus delivered a cocker spaniel to my family, but apparently Santa Claus forgot to deliver the Smith's dog on Christmas, because their dog came on New Year's

Day. Granted, it wasn't a cocker spaniel, but it was a dog nonetheless.

Regarding consumerism *Notre Dame Magazine* reported:

> Social status once depended on one's family name; however, the rise of consumerism in the United States gave rise to social mobility. With the increasing availability of goods, people became more inclined to define themselves by what they possessed and the subtle quest for higher status accelerated. Conspicuous consumption and materialism have been an insatiable juggernaut ever since.

Keeping up with the Joneses is alive and well, which is why targeting next-door neighbors of current customers is an effective way to sell products and services consistently from door to door. But to do it efficiently takes organization and determination to keep customer lists updated. It also may take several attempts at different times of the day and on different days of the week to catch next-door neighbors of customers at home. I remember having to return to one home that was sandwiched between two customers on seven different occasions before I finally was able to speak to the homeowner—but the extra effort paid off when they purchased the service.

Limiting Fall-Out

One of the worst feelings in door-to-door sales is driving home with no sales to show for your day's work.

This is especially true when you are only being paid in commissions. Over the years I've heard those dreadful days of no sales and no pay described by sales reps as "shooting blanks," "goose eggs," "bageling," and "getting a donut." But even worse than getting shut out for a day is finding out that one of your sales changed their mind and canceled the agreement or returned the product you sold them—an event referred to as *fall-out*. Thus, the time, effort, and energy that you put into making that sale is completely wasted, and more importantly, the commissions you thought you had earned are no more.

The feelings after *fall-out* would keep me awake at night, and I wanted to devise a plan that would help me to completely avoid it. After experiencing *fall-out* on a handful of occasions, I was determined to figure out how to steer clear of it happening again. But no matter what I tried, I learned that eliminating *fall-out* entirely was not possible unless I compromised on the number of accounts I was selling. I had to accept the fact that *fall-out* is just a part of sales. Although I couldn't avoid it altogether, I did come up with ways to limit *fall-out* and maintain a high level of production.

I believe that a 1-in-10 *fall-out* ratio is acceptable and encouraged. Think about it: sales reps who never sell customers who change their mind are just closing the easy sales. These sales reps are just picking off the low-lying fruit and missing out on sales that require more effort and skill. However, sales reps who are able to sway customers into making decisions they regret later are proving that they are able to close sales that others may not have.

However, if a sales rep's *fall-out* ratio exceeds 10 percent, then it's likely that they are not being up front with their customers, their products or services are not being delivered in a timely manner, and/or the sales rep is selling accounts in areas that have high cancel rates. Let's examine each of these possibilities in depth.

First, every aspect of the product or service must be reviewed in detail with the customer. It's important to be open and up front with customers about the particulars of the goods and services they are purchasing. Term length, return policy, penalty for early termination, and guarantees are just some of the items customers should be made aware of. Personally, I don't subscribe to the "get the signature and cross your fingers" approach to making sales. I would rather be up front with customers so they don't encounter any surprises once I've left.

Some sales reps are trained to avoid using the word "contract." I agree with this concept—to a point. The words "service agreement" or "service terms" are more pleasing to the ears of potential customers and denote the same meaning as "contract." However, if a customer ever asks if they are signing a contract, it should be made clear to them that they are.

If a customer asked me if they had to sign a contract, I might tell them, "This is a contract as long as we hold up our end of the bargain. We have agreed to provide you with a product, and as long as the product is functioning as I have explained, then there is a binding agreement."

It's also important to review other language in the contract that would assist the customer in understanding their obligation if the product or service isn't living up to the expectations that have been explained. Avoid overselling the product or service, and don't shy away from being straightforward. Sales reps that sell consistently sell solid accounts.

Second, do whatever possible to ensure the product or service you are selling is delivered or received the same day or next day. Customers should not be scheduled to receive products or services too far in advance because it increases the likelihood of them changing their mind and can also create scheduling conflicts.

If the customer requests to receive their products or services beyond the same day or next day, a sales rep should try to convince them not to do so. If they are going out of town, arrange for their items to be delivered to a neighbor or family member. If services are being rendered, complete whatever can be done on the exterior of their home and have them call for the inside portion of their service when they return. If inside services are necessary, have them make arrangements with a neighbor or family member to be at their home while service takes place.

This can actually be used as a selling point if it's explained to the customer as follows: "We do have to take care of installation either today or tomorrow, and that's why I'm able to offer you the discount. But if you can make arrangements to have somebody at the home while we do the installation, it will all be finished when you return."

If sales reps explain to their customers that the discount they are receiving is tied to the time frame when they receive their products or services, they will be much more willing to make arrangements to accommodate the time frame they are given.

Finally, sales reps should avoid selling in areas that have historically high cancellation rates. These areas can change over time and might vary from industry to industry, but high cancellation rates are most typical in low-income neighborhoods or areas that are highly transient, such as those around military bases or the corporate headquarters of large companies.

In one of my operations, we identified a highly transient city due to the number of military personnel living in the area. Before we knew much about the area, our sales reps had sold extremely well there, but we soon realized that the turnover of accounts in that city was causing more grief than good. Therefore, we prohibited our door-to-door sales reps from knocking doors there.

Management should be aware of the areas in their markets that have high *fall-out* rates. As these areas are identified, it's best for sales reps to steer clear of them and focus their time and attention working in areas where it's more likely they will get paid for what they sell.

To summarize, to be a consistent seller, you should view every contact as a potential customer, view every area as capable of producing sales, target next-door neighbors of customers, and limit *fall-out*. Ultimately these skills have a lot to do with working smart. And working smart, combined with working hard, is the lethal combination for producing sales at the highest level.

Chapter 5

What It Takes to Be Great

I'm always amazed at how easy it looks when professional baseball players hit home runs. The ball appears to launch off their bats even though their swing looks effortless.

I started playing baseball when I was eight years old and finished playing after I graduated from high school. During those ten years, I hit exactly zero home runs. No matter how hard I tried, I just couldn't hit one out of the park. And after all these years, I have come to realize that my problem was just that: I was trying too hard to hit the ball over the fence. Making sales is the same way. Trying too hard to sell something makes it more difficult to do, whereas those who are good at selling make it look easy.

I get a lot of satisfaction when making sales for reps while I'm training them on the doors. I especially enjoy hearing them say, as we are walking away from the customer's home, "That was an easy one. I could have sold them."

Because I've trained hundreds of sales reps, I realize that what they think they witnessed was nothing close to what had actually taken place. As roles are reversed and I begin observing them interacting with potential customers, my analysis is confirmed. Sales reps are too novice to realize that what they are doing doesn't compare in the slightest to what I did. What I say, how I say it, and even what I don't say is remarkably contrary to how my trainees communicate.

Similar to a baseball launching off a bat and sailing over the fence, the miniscule intricacies of bat speed, hip rotation, and proper balance required to make this happen go unnoticed by the average fan. In sales, the combination of what you say, how you say it, and what you don't say are the decisive elements that determine whether or not you get the sale.

Part I: What You Say

As I've already noted, the *Secret Sauce of Success* in sales is to be viewed as a messenger of good news and not as a salesperson. Therefore, what is said to potential customers must be the antithesis of what a stereotypical sales rep would say. The following are methods that demonstrate how to effectively come across as a messenger instead of as a sales rep:

- Questioning
- Sales Prostitute
- Yes Ma'am, No Ma'am

Questioning

There are three basic types of questions:

1. *Yes/No*
2. *Find-Out*
3. *Assumptive*

A *yes/no* question is the most elementary question and the most frequently asked. Sales reps commonly ask *yes/no* questions such as:

"Have you ever thought about buying this product before?"

"Is this service something you'd be interested in buying?"

"Will you sign up today?"

Yes/No questions aren't thought provoking for the potential customer and don't require much thought on the part of the sales rep either. Unfortunately, people are likely to respond to *yes/no* questions contrarily to what a sales rep hopes for, and once this happens, the conversation typically spirals downward and the sale is lost.

On rare occasions *yes/no* questions are appropriate to ask. If the person being spoken to isn't paying attention or being straightforward, a *yes/no* question might be asked to get their attention or flush out their concerns. For example:

"Did your neighbors tell you I would be coming by today?"

"Do you like living with pests in your home?"

However, for the most part, *yes/no* questions should be avoided.

Second is the *find-out* question. This type of question is more thought provoking than a *yes/no* question. *Find-Out* questions are open-ended and give the person being questioned an opportunity to answer with details. For example:

"What have you done in the past to maintain your yard?"

"What benefits do you think a security system offers your family?"

"What would you do with the time you'd be saving by having us clean your home?"

Effective *find-out* questions are supposed to do just that—help you find out more information. They allow the person being questioned to expound and provide information that can be helpful in knowing where to take the conversation. *Find-Out* questions, if asked correctly, can impact a sales rep's production positively.

Top sales reps ask *assumptive* questions because these types of questions can make the biggest impact on production. *Assumptive* questions are the highest level of questioning and the most difficult to formulate. People don't usually think to ask questions in assumptive ways, but *assumptive* questions allow you to lead people into making the decisions you want them to make. *Assumptive* questions are asked in a manner that the questioner assumes their audience will choose an option that is given. For example:

"Do you want us to clean the inside and outside of your windows, or just the outside?"

"Would you prefer we install your security system today or tomorrow?"

"Are you more concerned about landscaping your front yard or backyard?"

"Do you see more spiders inside your home or outside?"

The types of questions asked, directly relate to how effective sales reps are in receiving the answers they anticipate. Questions that are worded slightly differently can completely alter a discussion and be the determining factor as to whether the potential customer makes the purchase.

Properly asking questions doesn't just apply to sales. Effective questioning can also be a valuable tool in influencing others to do what you want them to do. Take, for example, the questions that could be offered when asking somebody on a date:

Yes/No: "Do you want to go out this Saturday?"

Find-Out: "What do you think about going out with me on Saturday?"

Assumptive: "Would you rather go out for steak or sushi when we go out Saturday?"

Notice how the *assumptive* question builds on the *yes/no* and *find-out* questions to help the questioner get the result they want. *Assumptive* questions lead people down a desired path, and if you're lucky, they might even lead you into getting a few more dates.

The door-to-door sales scene in the cinematic masterpiece *Napoleon Dynamite* perfectly depicts how ineffective questioning leads to a missed sales opportunity. Deb, Napoleon's friend, knocks on his door, and when he answers she attempts to sell him products and services that will help her earn money for college.

Deb: Um, hello. Would you like to look like this?

[*holds out a photo*]

Napoleon Dynamite: [*Napoleon takes the photo and looks at it*] This is a girl.

Deb: [*Deb continues nervously*] Because for a limited time only, Glamour Shots by Deb are 75 percent off.

Napoleon Dynamite: I already get my hair cut at the Cuttin' Corral.

Deb: Well, maybe you'd be interested in some home-woven handicrafts?

[*Scene continues*]

Deb: …And here we have some boondoggle key chains. A must-have for this season's fashion.

Napoleon Dynamite: I already made, like, infinity of those at scout camp.

Deb's debacle of an approach starts with a *yes/no* question that Napoleon misinterprets. He thinks she is offering him a haircut, when in reality she is trying to sell him a photo shoot. Instead of clarifying her intent, Deb attempts to sell Napoleon something else and asks yet another *yes/no* question. After Napoleon raises another objection, Deb figures she has lost the sale and shoves her caboodle full of boondoggle into Napoleon's arms and runs away, embarrassed and crestfallen. Her poor choice of questions lost her the sale, and you'll lose sales too by asking ineffective questions.

Sales Prostitute

A *sales prostitute* unashamedly succumbs to every wish and desire of their potential client in order to get the sale. Special requests are granted, accommodations are made, and rules are bent to satisfy the customer. For example:

> **Customer:** "Will you throw in an extra bottle of product for free?"
>
> **Sales Rep:** "Anything for you."
>
> **Customer:** "Can you also treat around our garage and play set for the same price?"
>
> **Sales Rep:** "For sure; no problem."
>
> **Customer:** "Will you include two more sensors in my home at no cost?"
>
> **Sales Rep:** "Absolutely. Whatever you want."

Sales prostitutes are desperate for sales, and their desperation might as well come in the form of perspiration because it's just as recognizable. Sales reps get taken advantage of once people know they are desperate. Potential customers will demand upgrades, increased guarantees, price reductions, free equipment, or anything else the sales rep is willing to give. And each time sales reps accommodate a request, their commissions (and dignity) become less significant.

By the way, *sales prostitutes* aren't doing the company they represent any favors either. Precedence has been set that the company will do whatever the customer demands, which generally leads to strained relationships between company and customer. However, there is justification for bending over backward for tenured customers that have brought value to the company because of their loyalty, a new client hasn't earned that privilege and the relationship will suffer if their every request is pandered to. In the end, such customers expect too much and are impossible to please.

Yes Ma'am, No Ma'am

The first cousin of a *sales prostitute* is the *yes ma'am, no ma'am* sales rep. This type of sales rep will immediately agree with what a potential customer wants to hear, rather than asking appropriate follow-up questions and educating the customer on important principles or policies. For example:

Customer: "Will this service get rid of all my spiders?"

Sales Rep: "Yes."

Customer: "Will your product clean the grease stains in my garage?"

Sales Rep: "Yes."

Customer: "Is your product harmful to pets?"

Sales Rep: "No."

Because they are agreeable, *yes ma'am, no ma'am* sales reps will likely produce sales, but the long-term prognosis for keeping their customers satisfied will be challenging. By failing to educate the customer, a *yes ma'am, no ma'am* sales rep typically oversells the product or service, and as a result, the company under-delivers on its end. In the long run, companies pay the price for their customers being uneducated and expecting the unrealistic.

Yes ma'am, no ma'am sales reps respond in fear of losing the sale instead of telling it like it is. Sales reps should not be afraid to tell people things that they may not want to hear. Doing so helps the sales rep earn the respect and trust of their potential customers. Instead of simply answering a question with a yes or no, answer with a question of your own. Doing so helps you find out more information that might be valuable to know as the potential customer progresses in the sale. For example:

> **Customer:** "Will this service get rid of all my spiders?"
>
> **Sales Rep:** "Where have you been noticing the spiders?"
>
> **Customer:** "Will your product clean the grease stains in my garage?"
>
> **Sales Rep:** "How long have you had the stains in your garage?"

Customer: "Is your product harmful to pets?"

Sales Rep: "What type of pets do you have?"

By responding to the person's question with a question, the sales rep is able to gather more information, which will help them to customize the product or service to better meet the needs of their potential customer. The sales technique of answering a question with a question is also an effective way to take back control of a conversation. Gaining and maintaining control of the conversation is a must if you want to become an effective salesperson.

Part II: How You Say It

How your voice sounds when it exits your lips is another way messages are sent and received during the sales process. This is referred to as meta verbal communication and includes voice characteristics such as volume, speed, pitch, and vocabulary.

Volume

As noted earlier, a sales rep's volume level is most effective at a seven. This level is loud enough that the sales rep will be paid attention to but soft enough that potential customers won't feel like they are being bombarded by a stereotypical salesperson.

It's important for sales reps to fluctuate their volume throughout the conversation. Speaking in a monotone voice can be irritating and boring to the potential customer. Changing up the volume assists in keeping the contact interested and helps the sales rep emphasize key points.

In short, a good mix of volume keeps the conversation interesting and holds the potential customer's attention long enough to make the points that need to be made.

Speed

People expect sales reps to talk quickly and rush through their sales pitch. And when this expectation is met, it's easy for potential customers to tune out the salesperson's message. Sales reps also talk quickly if they are nervous, lack confidence in what they are selling, or are afraid of silence.

A sales rep I trained in Albuquerque, New Mexico, learned the hard way why silence can be helpful while attempting to make a sale. The sales rep's initial approach began well enough, but instead of asking the customer a question or pausing to let her speak, he speedily rattled on about every policy, guarantee, and perk about the service he was selling.

As I observed the customer, I could tell she was getting impatient. She wanted to say something to the sales rep but didn't want to be rude and interrupt. The sales rep carried on for what seemed like an eternity, but in reality, hogged the conversation for about three minutes, before the customer finally reached her wits end and interrupted the sales rep, declaring, "I've wanted to tell you that I'm already a customer. I don't need you to sell me anything!"

The sales rep had been babbling incoherently to a current customer who wouldn't have bought the service from him no matter what he said to her. He could have found out she was a customer at the very beginning of the conversation if he had given her an opportunity to speak, but because he didn't, he wasted her time as well as his.

Besides being more conversational and sounding less like a salesperson, speaking at an even pace gives you the opportunity to think before you speak. This helps you more effectively structure sentences and formulate questions that will help you navigate potential customers along the path that leads them into buying your product or service.

It's also important to note that silence in conversation isn't necessarily a bad thing. Silent moments incite action from the person being spoken to. When a sales rep pauses, it indicates that it's time for the potential customer to respond. It almost forces them to say something. Pausing also communicates the authenticity of the message and that the sales rep values the potential customer's opinion.

A normally paced conversation is ideal in a sales setting because it makes the potential customer feel as though they are conversing with somebody who is sharing a message. They don't feel the pressure or tension that often accompany an interaction with a salesperson. As conversations flow naturally, sales are more likely to be made.

Pitch

The pitch of your voice helps potential customers formulate an image in their mind about who you are and what you represent. Pitch communicates the entire spectrum of emotions: happiness, anger, frustration, sadness, etc. Altering the pitch of your voice can cause the same sentence to be interpreted very differently. For example, say aloud the following question with a pitch that expresses anger:

"What are you doing?"

Now ask the same question with a joyful pitch. Although the words didn't change, your pitch significantly altered the meaning of the question.

A pitch problem that sales reps often make is singing their sentences. This is done by ending a sentence on a high note and is consistent with the pitch used when asking a question. Singing sentences communicates to the potential customer that you are questioning yourself and aren't knowledgeable or confident in the product or service you are selling.

In sales, the pitch of your voice must express confidence and dependability. Sentences should be stated confidently and end with the intended emphasis. Words that should be emphasized can be expressed emphatically or quietly, depending on the message.

Vocabulary

Confidence can also be communicated by taking ownership when speaking with potential customers. Avoid using phrases such as "the company" or "their employees." Once you wear their logo, you are that company so you should speak in terms of "my company" or "our employees." By taking ownership, you will be regarded as an expert by those you try to sell.

Certain words need to be avoided when talking with potential customers. If expressed, these forbidden words should signal sirens of warning to your mind. The list of outlawed vocabulary includes:

- *Problem*
- *Contract*
- *Selling/Signing Up*
- *Chemical*

The word *problem* should never be uttered in a sales setting. First of all, nobody likes to admit they have a problem and unless you're attending a meeting full of recovering addicts, it's highly unlikely that you will get potential customers to confess having problems, especially because you are likely to be meeting them for the first time.

It's important to understand that something viewed as a problem for one person could be viewed as ordinary for somebody else. Therefore, if you begin a conversation by saying, "I'm just in the neighborhood letting you know about the problem your neighbors are having with _____," it's likely that the person you are talking to, even if they have a problem, won't admit it. If that's the case, your conversation has ended.

While training a sales rep in Lancaster, California, we were knocking a neighborhood infested with tiny black ants. It was obvious that ants were a big *problem* in the area. And because the ants were so prevalent, it was fairly easy for my trainee to get the people he was contacting to admit to having an ant *problem*. During his opening line, he would tell potential customers that everybody in the area was having *problems* with ants and that he was there to take care of it.

As we approached the front door of one home, we noticed a stream of tiny black ants entering and exiting the home. A pheromone trail was leading these ants in a uniform manner back and forth from the house as if they were performing in a choreographed routine. There must have been thousands of them.

Noticing the ants, the sales rep began his approach the same way he had at the other homes in the neighborhood:

"Hello, sir. I'm in the neighborhood today because many of your neighbors are having a problem with black ants, and we are taking care of them."

To which the gentleman replied, "Well we don't have a problem, so I won't be needing your service."

The sales rep couldn't believe what he was being told. Here was a man claiming he didn't have a problem as ants steadily streamed into his home. The salesperson was at a loss for words and unsure how to respond. He gained his composure after stumbling over a few words, looked down at the ants in the doorway, and replied, "Well, there are little black ants everywhere in the neighborhood, and because of the problem, we are giving a big discount on our services."

The man once again disregarded the sales rep's comment and said, "I'm not interested…I don't have a problem."

At this point the sales rep became offended by the man's unwillingness to admit to an obvious problem. The sales rep then pointed down at the ants trafficking into the man's home and made the regrettable comment, "Well what are these then? Your neighbor's ants?"

Of course, this comment offended the potential customer and he quickly shut the door. This conflict could have easily been avoided if the sales rep hadn't used the word *problem* in his approach. He also could have pointed out the ants initially and let the gentleman know that the rest of the neighborhood was having the exact same type of ant activity.

But instead, the sales rep lost his composure and ultimately lost the sale when he assumed the man would admit to having a *problem*. Maybe pride, ignorance, or both cause people to avoid admitting to their *problems*. But regardless of the reason, using the word *problem* is a *problem* in and of itself.

Terms that can be used as substitutes for *problem* might include: issue, challenge, difficulty, circumstance, or situation. It's much easier for people to admit having difficulty or being challenged with something as opposed to admitting they have a *problem* with it.

The next word that should be avoided is *contract*. Isn't it true that most people avoid contracts like they would the plague? A *contract* is restrictive and banishes free will. It's no wonder they are evaded.

In place of *contract*, use the term *service agreement*. A *service agreement* connotes a two-way commitment between the parties involved. Thus, if one party delivers on their end of the agreement, the other party should deliver on theirs. A *service agreement* is team-oriented and sounds much nicer on the ears than does a *contract*.

Nevertheless, when a potential customer asks me if what they are signing is a *contract*, I will reply in the affirmative and then educate them on the terms of the *contract*. For example, if a product is guaranteed to do a certain thing but doesn't deliver, then the customer should have some sort of recourse because the product didn't live up to the expectation.

So, I might tell the customer, "This is a contract, but you are only obligated to the agreement if the product you are purchasing does what I've explained it will do. If the product fails to do this, then you can return the product as outlined in the agreement."

Likewise, if a service is offered but doesn't deliver as outlined in the agreement, the customer should have safeguards to ensure their satisfaction. These safeguards might come as additional services or a money-back guarantee; whatever the case may be, it's important to be forthright with the customer so they are clear on the terms of the *contract*.

The next terms to avoid are *selling* or *signing up*. Generally, people are very hesitant to confess they have been sold something. They would much rather admit that they purchased a product or service on their terms and not somebody else's. Therefore, sales reps should avoid making comments such as:

"I'm in the neighborhood *selling* this product that is…"

"The service I'm *selling* to your neighbors..."

"I'm in the neighborhood *signing up* people..."

These statements are likely to turn off potential customers to your message. Remember: as a messenger of good news you aren't *selling* or *signing up* anybody, you are simply delivering a message and letting them make up their own minds about what actions to take.

When knocking doors and speaking with potential customers, some will immediately ask, "What are you selling?"

To which you could respond by saying, "Actually I just finished talking with Ryan (*name of the nearest neighbor*), and I'm just letting everybody know what's going on in the neighborhood. Did anybody tell you I would be stopping by?"

This response might come as a relief to the potential customer because you don't appear to be a salesperson, but simply a messenger passing on information that has been given to other neighbors. You will find potential customers much more responsive to somebody delivering information to them as opposed to *selling* them something.

The term *signing up* also comes across too salesy. A stereotypical salesperson lets their contacts know they are *signing up* the neighbors for a service or that a bunch of people have *signed up* to receive their product. The term *signing up* also implies having to sign something, possibly a *contract*, which gives more reason to avoid using this term. Good substitutes for *signing up* could be: setting up, servicing, supplying, or providing.

A final word to avoid using is *chemical*. If the products or services you are selling are composed of or involve the use of *chemicals*, it's best to substitute the word *product* instead. The word *chemical* does not come across positively in any context. It conjures up images of skulls, crossbones, and hazmat crews in yellow space suits. If a potential customer ever feels that the products or services you are offering will pose a threat to them, the sale will not be made.

However, if what is being sold involves the use of *chemicals*, there is absolutely no circumstance when a sales rep is justified in telling a potential customer that the products being used are safe. *Chemicals* aren't safe, but if their labels are followed correctly, then they will serve the purpose for which they are intended.

Mirroring Tone

Mirroring the tone of potential customers is a technique intended to gain their respect. If a potential customer talks softly, the sales rep should speak softly. If the customer takes on more of an aggressive tone, that tone should be mirrored as well.

While knocking doors in Santa Rosa, California, an exceptionally grumpy old man answered his door and instantly shouted at me, "I'm not interested!"

A little taken aback at first, I realized I wasn't dealing with the typical contact, so I mirrored his tone and barked back, "Well I guess your neighbors haven't told you what I'm doing out here then."

Immediately following my words, his facial expression softened, his eyes opened a bit wider, and he inquiringly uttered, "Uh, no, they haven't. What's going on?"

I proceeded to tell him about the discounted service I was offering his neighbors, and to my surprise, after a lengthy conversation, he ended up signing a service agreement.

I had a similar experience while working in Jacksonville, Florida. I was knocking doors in a neighborhood that had been having issues with scorpions. In fact, after speaking with one of the neighbors, I learned that a six-year-old boy had been stung by a scorpion only a few days prior to my arrival. It was fairly easy to get the attention of the neighbors being that most of them knew about this young boy's incident.

However, some weren't privy to the news, and one man in particular opened his door and with a scowl that would have frightened the Grim Reaper shouted, "What are you doing here?"

To which I shouted back: "Haven't you heard?"

He responded, and our shouting match continued. "Heard about what?"

Continuing to mirror his tone, I said, "One of your neighbors' kids was stung by a scorpion, and I'm here to make sure nobody else gets stung."

Upon hearing my retort, the man's body language changed entirely. His shoulders rolled forward; he leaned closer to me and said in a whisper, "I've been seeing them too. Come inside and let me show you where."

As I entered the man's home, he couldn't have been more cordial. He offered me something to drink and showed me all of the areas in his home where he'd encountered the stinging arachnids. Although our conversation started out as a shouting match, it ended with the man agreeing to become a customer. This outcome was made possible because I mirrored his tone and stood my ground instead of wilting under his initial brashness.

Chris S., a former sales rep of mine, used a similar technique as he encountered people who seemed annoyed by his presence. If a homeowner came to the door and acted put off by his being there, he would tell them in an irritated tone, ["I'm sorry to bother you, but my boss is making me come out here today and I'm not too happy about it. I'm supposed to tell you what's going on in your neighborhood..."] *Mimic grumpy*

After continuing to explain the service he was offering, Chris often found that the person's mood about his being there would change. In fact, some people would relate to Chris by sharing their challenges of having to work for a boss who required them to do something they were opposed to.

No matter your contact's initial temperament, you can get on their good side by making efforts to mirror their tone. This may be challenging at first because it's easy to get into a routine of saying what you normally say, how you typically say it. However, breaking out of your comfort zone and mirroring the tone of your potential customers will enable you to become more of a messenger and less of a salesperson.

Water It Down

The final technique to note in regards to "How You Say It" is knowing how and when to *water it down*. As a child I had the hardest time choking down cough syrup when I wasn't feeling well. My mom would threaten to hold me down and force me to drink it if every last drop didn't make its way down my throat. And once the tiny plastic cup was emptied, she always gave me the same advice: "Water it down."

I would immediately go to the cupboard, grab the tallest glass, and fill it to the brim. I'd chug the entire glass of water to make sure the aftertaste of cough syrup didn't linger in my mouth. Relatedly, sales reps can leave a bad taste in the mouths of their potential customers by asking them to open their wallets and spend money on products and services. Therefore, watering down certain aspects of what is being sold is an important sales tactic that helps the thought of making a purchase more palatable.

The idea behind watering it down is to describe the worst-case scenario to the potential customer and then explain how your offer is a better alternative. There are three items that should be watered down while attempting to make a sale: price, duration of agreement, and amount to purchase/frequency of visits.

1. Price

If you are offering your products or services at a discount, watering down the price is simple. I recommend using a pricing sheet that shows the normal rates for what you are selling. A pricing sheet legitimizes the discount by showing what the potential customer would have to pay for the products or services if they chose to buy them at a later date.

Pricing sheets should be visually appealing. The more official-looking the pricing sheet, the more the potential customer will believe that the discount you are offering is a better option. Effectively watering down the price to a potential customer could be done as follows:

(While showing them the pricing sheet) "As you can see, the normal price for this product is $____. You can call the office to get this price anytime, but while I'm in the neighborhood today, I can offer it for $____."

Potential customers are far more likely to believe that the discount you are offering is authentic if you have a pricing sheet that stands as a second witness to what you are telling them. By using a pricing sheet, you can effectively water down the price of the product or service you are selling.

2. Duration of Agreement

It's imperative to water down the duration of an agreement if the service you are selling requires a certain time commitment. The actual time frame of the commitment is irrelevant. What's important is that the duration, whatever it might be, is watered down.

For example, if you were selling a window cleaning service and the commitment was for twelve months, you might explain:

"To offer you this discount, we are setting the neighbors up on just our starter program. This isn't one of those three- to five-year commitments, of course (shaking your head back and forth). The starter program is just for one year."

If you were selling a home security system, you might explain:

"Some companies require that they monitor your system for up to five years, but the great thing about my offer is that you only have to commit to three years of monitoring."

halfly, Sen Dayor plus

When sales reps effectively outline the worst-case scenario, their contacts will be grateful for the opportunity to agree to a lesser commitment. Effectively watering down the duration of the agreement will give your potential customers the relief of knowing they can "try it out" before committing to something long-term.

3. Amount to Purchase/Frequency of Visits

You might be selling a product that needs to be sold in certain quantities for the customer to receive the best price, or a service you are selling might require a specific number of visits for the customer to realize the best discount. Either way, watering down these terms is a necessity to entice more people to buy what you are selling.

If you were selling a set of kitchen knives, you might explain to a potential customer:

"For the half-price discount I'm able to offer today, you only have to purchase one complete set of knives. Normally, for this type of pricing, you have to buy multiple sets."

If you were selling a seasonal fertilizing service, you might say:

"The good news is that we aren't going to be fertilizing your yard every week or two (shaking your head back and forth). We fertilize your yard every six weeks throughout the spring, summer, and fall seasons, which is great because this program saves you a lot of money too."

Watering down the amount of products or frequency of visits are great ways to paint the picture of what the potential customer might have to endure if they wait to purchase what you are selling. It's important to communicate a sense of urgency in your offer to entice your contacts into action.

So you see, watering it down is an effective sales method to help potential customers understand that they shouldn't postpone what they are considering purchasing. As a messenger and not a salesperson, you are sharing good news by offering best-case scenarios that assist others in purchasing products and services under the best terms, for the best prices.

Part III: What You Don't Say

Nonverbal communication studies have made claims that nonverbal communication makes up about 66 percent of all communication (Hogan and Stubbs 2003). Nonverbal messages are sent in a variety of ways, some of which include body position, eye contact, facial expressions, hand movement, and appearance.

During the sales process, your words can communicate one message, but nonverbally, you could be communicating something completely different. For example, your words say, "The service I am offering is the best in the industry, and with the discount I'm offering you won't find a better offer."

However, if you're saying this while looking away, shuffling your feet, or having timid facial expressions, there is no way the person you are talking to will believe you. Having good nonverbal communication skills will build your confidence and create an expectation of hearing "yes" at every sales opportunity.

The following pages will outline effective and ineffective ways to communicate nonverbally in a sales setting:

Body Position

Standing with your shoulders squared up to a potential customer may give an impression of intimidation, similar to a boxing match when the two opponents stand toe to toe in the center of the ring. You should never attempt to sell your product or service by intimidation. Instead, when standing in front of a contact, turn your body slightly, in a relaxed manner, to communicate approachability and geniality.

One Saturday while shopping for a leather recliner, my wife and I visited a furniture store near our home. The salesperson who greeted us had a habit of standing squarely in front of us at an uncomfortably close distance. Even as we tried to move away from him, he continued to follow us and keep himself directly in front of us. Although he spoke kindly, his poor choice of body position made him an unintended threat. Each time he came closer to us, we found ourselves retreating, until eventually I asked him to let us continue shopping on our own.

As we left the store and were walking back to the car, my wife proclaimed, "That guy made me nervous."

By no means was the sales rep physically intimidating, but his poor body language made him a threat to us—and he ultimately lost a sale because of it.

Eye Contact

There is no exact formula for how long you should maintain eye contact with somebody. A good rule of thumb is to hold a gaze for just a few seconds and then look away for about half that time.

If you've ever had the experience of talking with somebody who stares, you know how uncomfortable that is. You don't even want to look back into the person's eyes knowing that their piercing stare will be looking right through you. As a sales rep, winning a staring contest with your potential customers will not guarantee you a signed agreement.

On the other hand, avoiding eye contact makes you appear weak and shows a lack of confidence in what you are selling. It's difficult to determine if the person in front of you is paying attention to what you are saying if they fail to give any eye contact. It's almost like having a conversation with yourself.

Facial Expressions

A potential customer should never catch you off guard with a comment or question. No matter what comes out of their mouth, you have to act as though it's something you've heard time and time again. If they think they have said something that surprises you, your credibility is instantly minimized.

A confident sales rep will always have a smile unless the conversation turns serious. A smile has the ability to put a potential client at ease and remove any tension they may be feeling about conversing with a sales rep. It's important to keep a smile even if you are thinking about what you want to say next. Your contact will appreciate it if you are attentively listening to what they are saying. Most importantly a smile exudes confidence in yourself and what you are selling.

Head Nod

When you want the potential customer to agree with you, nod your head up and down or shake it back and forth. For example:

"What your neighbors have liked about our group rate discount is you don't have to sign up for two or three years (shaking your head back and forth). Instead, you can start with the one-year service plan (nodding your head up and down) to see if you like it."

If the person you are talking to begins to mirror your head nod, they are nonverbally communicating trust in you and what you are telling them.

It's also appropriate to head nod while a potential customer is speaking to acknowledge that you are either agreeing or disagreeing with what they are saying. It's a joy to talk with somebody who nods their head when you are talking to them because it communicates that they are intently following your every word. Sales reps who effectively head nod while in conversation with potential customers earn their respect and admiration.

Hand Movement

Using your hands effectively will take attention off of your face and make what you are saying more interesting. Move your hands to illustrate certain aspects of your product or service:

If you are selling a security system, use your fist to show how an intruder could break the glass of a window to get into the person's home.

If you are selling a pest control service, you could hold your hand in a fist and open all your fingers and wiggle them to demonstrate how a spider's egg sac hatches and the baby spiders start crawling.

If you are selling a lawn care service, use your hands and fingers to show how the fertilizer time releases once it has interacted with moisture.

Another effective hand movement is to use your fingers to point out the homes of neighbors who have purchased your product or service. As you use their neighbors' names and point to their homes, the potential customer will be sure to follow your gesture.

Mirroring

As noted earlier, mirroring is when one person's actions are reflected by another. To me, mirroring is how potential customers give *tells*. A *tell*, in poker terms, is a nonverbal clue given by an opponent that helps to determine whether the person is holding good cards. For example, if a card player is observed as stoic throughout the game and then suddenly hints at a smile, the *tell* might be that he has been dealt a good hand.

If a potential customer mirrors my actions, that is my *tell* to know they trust me and are likely to purchase what I'm selling. My favorite *tell* is the doorframe lean. During my conversation I will intentionally lean my shoulder on the person's doorframe, and if they mirror me by leaning on the other side of their doorframe, it's almost certain they will purchase what I am selling.

When you head nod and your potential customers head nod back, they are communicating trust in what you are telling them. Conversely, you nonverbally communicate trust in your potential customers when you mirror their actions. For example, if they laugh, laugh with them; if they fold their arms, fold yours; if they have a scowl on their face, have one of yours too. Mirroring others is a way to nonverbally communicate that you are on the same page with them. It's as though you are teammates working together in an effort to accomplish the same goal.

Appearance

As a salesperson, always look professional. Unkempt hair (including unkempt facial hair), an untucked shirt, distracting jewelry, and tattoos can all be the means of sidetracking people from focusing on your message. Some appearance flaws even increase the odds that others won't trust you. Successful sales reps make it a point to look professional no matter what they are selling.

Admittedly I'm not a fan of the New York Yankees. I am, however, a big fan of the Yankees' grooming standards, which were instituted by their late owner George Steinbrenner. Mr. Steinbrenner won seven World Series titles over the thirty-seven years he owned the team, and one of his well-known but not necessarily well-liked policies was his military-style grooming code.

This policy prohibits all Yankees players, coaches, and executives from having any facial hair, other than a well-groomed mustache, and the hair on their heads can't be grown below their collars. Over the years the baseball club has signed players who have blatantly broken these grooming standards while playing for other teams; however, as soon as they become New York Yankees, their hair is neatly trimmed and their faces cleanly shaven. With a razor and a pair of scissors, the Yankees transform a trashy look to a classy one.

Sales reps would do themselves a lot of good by adhering to the Yankees' grooming standards but some think that looking "cool" and "in style" is more important than looking professional and dignified. These are typically the sales reps that aren't as successful as they could and should be. The reality is that potential customers are more likely to buy from sales reps who not only act the part but also look the part. There is no question that sales can either be helped or hindered strictly based on appearance.

As a sales rep, the company you represent should be prominently displayed on clothing and sales materials. I suggest having your company's logo visible in at least three different places, such as a hat, shirt, identification badge, sales binder, or other promotional material.

I am extremely superstitious when it comes to my appearance as a sales rep. When I worked as a full-time door-to-door salesman, I had specific shirts that I'd wear on specific days, a certain brand and color of shoe I had to wear while knocking, and even a specific type of click-pen I would use to fill out service agreements. One summer, I even painted my fingernails with a clear, glossy nail polish to improve the appearance of my fingers... and in case you're wondering, yes, my wife still gives me a hard time for doing that.

Sales reps who take pride in their appearance will radiate confidence in themselves and what they are selling. The people they talk to will hold them in higher regard because they look the part. And at the end of the day, an impressive appearance translates into making more sales.

Visual Aids

Sometimes showing somebody something is easier than trying to explain it. If the company you work for has visual aids, you should use them throughout your sales pitch. Pictures bring life to the products and services you are selling and make it easier for people to visualize what they are buying.

Proper use of pictures also takes the spotlight off of you and gives the potential customer something else to focus on. It's not that you aren't interesting or good looking, but if a picture is worth a thousand words, let it do the talking for you.

Filler Words

Words such as "um," "like," and "but" should be erased from your vernacular because they convey nervousness and uncertainty about the message you are sharing. And besides, the excessive use of filler words is incredibly annoying.

While on an airplane flying to Boise, Idaho, I sat behind a couple of Boise State University students who were returning to school after summer break. As I overheard them talking to each other, it became obvious that one of them had a serious filler word problem. Her dialog went something like this:

"I was, like, back at home, and, like, my mom was like, 'Why are you so, like, bored to be here at our house?' And I was like, 'Mom, like, you don't understand. It's not like all my friends are here.'"

After a couple of minutes of, like, hearing her, like, speak this way, I put on my noise-cancelling headphones to relieve my ears of the horrendous babble coming out of the coed's mouth.

It's often difficult for the person using filler words to recognize them. It's not a bad idea to practice your approach with a friend, spouse, or colleague to make sure no filler words are creeping into your sales pitch.

To sum up, "What You Don't Say" during a conversation isn't exactly rocket science, but it is a science nonetheless. There are proven theories and laws that work when speaking to others, and these laws act just like physical laws. If used correctly, they work every time. OK. Maybe not every time, but if used correctly, they have a high probability of success.

Effective nonverbal communication is a two-way street. As a sales rep you have to be aware of every minor detail of how you are communicating nonverbally. Is your body slightly turned? Do you look professional? Are you head nodding? Are you using your hands? All of these things matter when talking with potential customers, and even the slightest errors can be costly.

Equally important to recognizing your own nonverbal communication is being able to understand what nonverbal cues the person in front of you is signaling. Are they folding their arms because they feel threatened? If so, put something in their hand like a picture of your product or pricing sheet. Are they nodding their head in agreement as you are making a point? If so, they probably believe what you are telling them. Understanding what your potential customers are communicating nonverbally will help you to know if "What You Say" and "How You Say It" are in alignment with "What You Don't Say."

Chapter 6

Forty-Five Seconds

Immediately after making eye contact with a potential customer, the forty-five-second clock begins. This is how much time you have as a sales rep to communicate, both verbally and nonverbally, a compelling statement that will earn you more time with a potential customer. These precious seconds, known as an initial approach, can either make or break the sale.

Forty-five seconds is long enough to prove that what you are selling can bring value to the person standing in front of you but short enough to keep their attention and not allow them enough time to think of a reason to reject your offer. By keeping the initial approach brief, you also show respect for the potential customer's time, and you demonstrate how valuable your time is as well.

Similar to my experience in Albuquerque, New Mexico, with the sales rep who rambled on for minutes not knowing he was talking to a current customer, is an experience I had while observing a sales rep in Aurora, Colorado. This sales rep's initial approach was carrying on for much longer than the suggested forty-five seconds, and as I observed the potential clients she was talking to, it became evident they were bothered by her unwillingness to let them speak. During one conversation in particular, she learned why keeping her initial approach brief is so important.

A man came to the door, and the sales rep began her initial approach by talking about the company she worked for. Then she told him about the discount she was offering, followed by a description of the service, the terms of the service guarantee, and even the details of the company's cancellation policy.

After a few minutes, the sales rep paused just long enough so the man could sneak in a few words of his own. He proceeded to tell us that he was already a customer and had been for several years. He said that he was quite aware of most everything the sales rep was telling him. However, he was intrigued by the "discount" she mentioned and wanted to know the specifics.

The sales rep told him what the discounted price was, and come to find out, the price she was offering his neighbors was lower than what he was paying. He rightly became bothered at this news and consequently called into the office demanding the discounted price his neighbors were being offered. He argued that he should be rewarded for his years of loyalty, and the company agreed. His request was honored and his price was lowered.

None of this would have happened if the sales rep's initial approach had been succinct. If she would have given the customer time to speak before rambling on, he would have been able to identify himself as a current customer and the particulars of the discount would have never been mentioned.

Sales reps must stay on task and only share the pertinent information that will assist them in determining whether their time is best spent with the person in front of them. The following should be addressed during the initial approach and if followed, these points will keep the initial approach around forty-five seconds and give the sales rep enough time to explain what they are selling.

- Who are you?
- Why are you there?
- What are you offering?
- Closing question.

Who Are You?

First, as is customary in most parts of the world, when you meet somebody for the first time, you introduce yourself. As a sales rep, it's appropriate to introduce who you are and the company you represent:

"Hello. My name is Tess, and I'm with AAA Home Security..."

Easy enough, right? Although basic, this is an effective way to introduce who you are. As you become more comfortable with your role as a sales rep and the company you work for, you could also insert some personality while explaining who you are:

"Hello. My name is Jackson, and I'm the bug guy with Mountain West Pest Control. I was sent here to bug you today…"

"Hi. I'm Abby, the best-looking door-to-door salesgirl you've ever had knock your door…"

If you attempt to inject personality into your initial approach, it must be genuine. Potential customers will easily recognize forced or phony approaches, and you will come across as a stereotypical sales rep.

Why Are You There?

Next, explain why you are there. As noted earlier, *name-dropping* gives you a legitimate reason to be on the doorstep and makes you appear as a messenger, not a salesperson. After *name-dropping*, you can gauge the person's interest with an appropriate *yes/no* question, such as:

"I was just talking to the Cutler family next door. Did anybody in the area mention I'd be stopping by?"

Besides gauging interest, this question is also designed to get the potential customer's attention. If they appear disinterested or distracted, a *yes/no* question will force them into the conversation. The potential customer will likely say they haven't been notified by their neighbors, and you can proceed by explaining:

"Just really quickly, I wanted to make sure everybody in the neighborhood knows what's going on…"

Although *name-dropping* in this fashion is effective, even better is to use the names of current customers. And even better than using current customers' names is showing the paperwork of customers you've recently sold.

For example, if I had just sold a product to the Cardwell family and had their signed paperwork in hand, when approaching their neighbors, I would introduce myself and then briefly show the person the Cardwell's paperwork, just long enough so they could see the name, then tuck the paperwork away and continue by saying:

"I just finished setting up an appointment with the Cardwell family, and they wanted me to let their neighbors know what we are going to be doing for them…"

By briefly showing the Cardwells' contract to their neighbors, I have accomplished two things. First, I will not be viewed as a random salesperson because I have established a legitimate reason for contacting them. And second, the person is more likely to purchase my products because of the *bandwagon effect* noted earlier.

Up to this point of the initial approach, you should come across as 100 percent messenger and 0 percent salesperson—meaning you have them right where you want them.

What Are You Offering?

The third step of the initial approach is to explain what you are offering. Think Black Friday. Remember: you are offering a discount that must be exclusive and must have an expiration date. Your conversation might continue as follows:

"Because I already have deliveries scheduled in your neighborhood tomorrow, I would like to keep my delivery truck in the area, so I am offering a huge discount for the next two orders I am able to fill…"

Or you might say:

"Since we will be servicing the Hancock home tomorrow, I have a couple of time slots available for two more neighbors that I can offer for half the price while we are in the area…"

By keeping the offer exclusive and including an expiration date, you have set the parameters for the sale. If the person wants to take advantage of your offer, they must do so according to your constraints. This method is as anti-salesperson as it gets. You aren't being a *sales prostitute* or a *yes ma'am, no ma'am* sales rep. You are being what you should be: a messenger. And a messenger who delivers information has a far better chance of making sales than does a stereotypical salesperson.

Closing Question

The final piece of an effective initial approach is the closing question, which can be asked in three different ways.

1. Soft Close
2. Hard Close
3. Conversational Close

The most effective close is the conversational close. My favorite conversational close is:

"How long have you lived in the area?"

This simple close accomplishes several goals:

*   It's conversational so it doesn't sound like you are selling anything
*   It gives the potential customer an opportunity to speak
*   It's a nonthreatening question that is easily answered
*   When you know how long the person has lived in their home, you can customize an explanation of why your product or service is perfect for them

The following are examples of other effective conversational closes:

"Did you buy the home when it was first built, or have there been previous owners?"

"What year was your home built?"

"How many times has a housecleaning company (or whatever type of company you represent) come by your home since you've lived here?"

The main purpose of asking a conversational close is to gather information that will help you to tailor the benefits and usefulness of your product or service as you continue the conversation.

Soft closes are more direct than conversational closes and are designed to call the potential customer to action. Soft closes should not be *yes/no* questions but should give the contact a choice between two viable options. The following are examples of effective soft closes:

"I could have my technician here tomorrow before noon or sometime after five. What works best for you?"

"The discount I'm offering could include cleaning the inside and outside of your windows, or you could just have the outsides cleaned. What option works best for you?"

Soft closes are great for flushing out potential customer concerns. After forty-five seconds, there is little hope that the person will be ready to purchase your product or service, so soft closes give them an opportunity to explain why they aren't interested in what you are selling. There is no reason to stall the inevitability of a concern, and soft closes get concerns out into the open sooner rather than later.

Hard closes are most effectively used by confident and/or desperate sales reps. Confident sales reps have little doubt the person in front of them will buy what they are selling. Their confidence is built from past success, and they have no problem using hard closes to quickly determine whether the potential customer is interested.

Sales reps might become desperate if they haven't achieved their daily sales goal and are running out of daylight. A hard close lets the sales rep know right away whether the person they are talking to is worthy of their limited time. The following are examples of hard closes:

"Can you have everything ready for us to clean your carpets by 4:00 p.m. tomorrow?"

"If you want to take advantage of the discount, I can reserve you a spot; if not, I will give it to one of your neighbors."

Hard closes can also be used when a conversation becomes stagnant. If you're unsure whether the potential customer intends to buy what you are selling, offer a hard close to determine whether you are spending time with a potential sale. Hard closing is about finding people who are interested without wasting time on those who aren't.

It doesn't seem appropriate that a chapter titled Forty-Five Seconds took almost two thousand words to define, but effective initial approaches have many particulars and moving parts. The actual words said are certainly important; however, the most important aspects of initial approaches are making sure the words are said conversationally and confidently.

Chapter 7

Qualifying

Once you've finished your initial approach, the next step is finding out whether the potential customer qualifies for more of your time. Yes, that is written correctly; they must qualify for more of your time, not the reverse. Your time is too valuable to be wasted, and it makes no sense to spend time with people who give no indication of interest.

When to continue a conversation or end one can be difficult to determine. During my years of training, I've observed numerous sales reps continue conversations with people who would never buy; conversely, I've witnessed just as many end conversations with people sincerely interested in buying. So how do you know when it's the right time to end a conversation or if you should continue trying to make a sale? The bottom line is that potential customers must qualify for your time.

I have identified four qualifiers that will assist you in knowing whether a person has a genuine interest in what you are selling. Keep in mind, not all four qualifiers need to be brought up for a potential customer to earn more of your time. One will do. But no matter how many qualifiers surface, once a qualifier has been revealed, you have the green light to continue trying to sell your product or service. The following are the four qualifiers:

1. If the potential customer asks, "How much is it?"
2. If the potential customer asks questions about your product or service
3. If the potential customer already owns the product or uses the service you are selling
4. If you observe a need for the product or service you are selling

1. How Much Is It?

Having sold products and services to thousands of people, I can guarantee that during the course of any sale I've ever made, the customer has asked me how much what I'm selling costs. Thus, I have deduced from my experience that it's essential for people to know how much something costs before making a purchase. Therefore, if the cost is asked, it's a guarantee that there is some level of interest. It may only be an ounce of interest, but there is interest nonetheless. This is why emphasizing a discount during the initial approach is so important. If the potential customer has absolutely no interest, the mention of a discount will fall on deaf ears.

By way of example, suppose I was looking to buy a new pair of men's dress shoes. Upon walking into the shoe store, a salesperson approaches me and says:

"Just letting you know that women's pumps are ninety percent off."

If I have no interest in purchasing a pair of women's pumps, I would probably acknowledge that I heard what the salesperson said and then ask where I could find the selection of men's dress shoes.

By the way, any shoe salesperson who approaches a potential customer, man or woman, and uses the previously noted initial approach could quite possibly be the worst salesperson of all time. Knowing what you know about initial approaches from the previous chapter, you of course would approach a potential shoe-buying customer and say:

"Thanks for coming in. I'm Tammy. Just to let you know, a number of our shoes are half price today. Are you looking for more of an outdoor shoe or an indoor shoe?"

But I digress.

In the same scenario, let's suppose the shoe salesperson approaches me and says:

"Today a number of our men's basketball shoes are half price."

In this case, I might have enough interest in men's basketball shoes to at least ask which shoes are half-price and how much they cost. Even though my intent is to buy men's dress shoes, it would be difficult to pass up a great deal for something I may eventually have an interest in purchasing.

When a potential customer asks how much your product or service costs, it should sound like music to your ears. But just because the question is asked doesn't mean the sale is imminent. There is still a long way to go, but at least the person has qualified for more of your time.

If cost is queried, the next step is making sure your product or service is explained in detail before offering up the price. Building value in what you are selling will help to justify its cost. If you reveal the cost immediately, the person may not have enough information to make an educated decision on your product or service's intrinsic value.

To properly build value in what you are selling, it's imperative to know as much as you can about your product or service. The more you know, the more you will be respected and trusted by your potential customers. And once you've earned their respect and trust, the probability of them buying from you increases dramatically.

Somebody who became extremely successful in large part because of the effort he put into knowing as much as he could about what he was selling was the late Larry H. Miller. Miller built a multibillion-dollar empire consisting of car dealerships, restaurants, professional sports franchises, movie theaters, TV and radio stations, and several other ventures (nearly ninety companies in all). Working in a car parts store in his early twenties, Miller dedicated himself to learning as much as he possibly could about car parts. His knowledge eventually gained him international recognition and launched his career in the car industry.

As a stock boy, he observed countermen needing to refer to catalogs to find specific parts. He was convinced that the process could become more proficient. He started memorizing car parts in catalogs and until his dying day could tell you the ten-digit stock number of any part of a Toyota vehicle. He could take any make of Toyota and build a vehicle one piece at a time with those stock numbers.

From his autobiography, *Driven*:

What I realized was that if you memorized the number system of the parts, rather than look them up in a catalog, you would be able to find things quickly and help more customers more efficiently. The other guys were spending too much time looking in the catalog. Instead of having my nose buried in a catalog, I decided I would interact with people.

I realized - if I took the time to study the catalogs, there were patterns that could make it easy to memorize parts numbers. So I began to memorize the parts numbers and their locations. I would go to bed each night and see catalog pages in my head listing fuel pumps and filters and gaskets, and I couldn't shake it.

(Customers) were always needing custom fittings, elbows, sleeves, compression fittings, flare nuts, that kind of thing. That's when I decided to sit down and understand the different types of threads, connecting systems, elbows and compression unions so that I could properly serve these customers. It was fun solving their problems.

When people came in with grease up to their elbows and frustration on their faces and asked if I knew how they could connect certain parts, I was able to say, "Yeah, you take this, connect one of these and this to that, you need an elbow here, a compression fitting here, and you've got it." They thought I was brilliant, and I had a lot of fun.

When I was behind a parts counter and heard a customer describe a problem or a list of symptoms, I could diagnose the source of the problem even from behind the counter... my knowledge of cars was very helpful. (Miller 2012, 75, 183)

Because of his extensive knowledge, Miller gained the respect and trust of his peers and clients. Knowledge truly is power when it comes to being successful at sales. Whatever it is you are selling, take time to learn as much as you can about your product or service.

When a potential customer qualifies by asking the cost of what you are selling, you must be able to build value in the product or service before revealing the price. Detailed descriptions and visual aids also help in building value. Once you have thoroughly explained your product or service, you should then reveal the price. Potential customers should only have to ask once how much your product or service costs. After you've built up the value, don't wait for them to ask again; proceed with a price quote.

2. What Does It Do?

Another qualifier occurs when a potential customer asks questions about your product or service. Questions such as:

"What exactly does your product do?"

"How does your service work?"

"How does your product compare to what I can buy in the store?"

"Is your service safe for my pets?"

These types of questions are proof that the person has interest in what you are selling and therefore qualifies for more of your time. If potential customers ask questions about your product or service, don't wait for them to ask how much the service costs. You can reveal the price after you have built value into what you're selling. Once again, the more you know about your product or service the better equipped you will be to answer questions in a convincing manner.

3. We Already Have That

The third qualifier is when your contact already owns the product or uses the service you are selling. For instance, if you are selling a home security system, and you come to a home that already has a security sign in their front yard, this is a great sign (literally) that the homeowner qualifies for your time because they already see the value in a home security system. Or, if you were selling a fertilizing service and noticed a lawn flag indicating that a person's lawn had recently been fertilized, you would most certainly want to talk to the homeowners. In fact, many companies leave signs, stickers, or other indicators on their customers' property for marketing purposes—but for door-to-door sales reps, these items act as qualifying targets. Once you know the homeowners already have what you are selling, then your job is to prove to them why your product or service is superior to what they already own or use.

The following three steps will help you convince the person you are talking with to buy what you are selling— even if they already have it.

Step 1

Acknowledge the person's wisdom for owning the product or service you are selling. If I were selling a lawn-mowing service and a potential customer told me they already had somebody taking care of that service for them, I might respond by saying:

"I'm glad you see the value of having somebody take care of your lawn-mowing needs. It's one of those things that it's hard to find the time to do..."

Notice that I didn't ask what company they were using or how much they were being charged. I'll find that out later. Initially I complimented them on their decision to use a lawn-mowing service.

Instead of expressing approval for their decision, suppose I told them that the lawn-mowing service they were using wasn't doing a good job because of the uneven edges and crooked lines in their lawn. There's a good chance this would offend the potential customer because I questioned their decision making when selecting a lawn-mowing company. They might also become defensive because I insulted their intelligence for choosing a company that wasn't doing a good job. If a potential customer ever becomes offended or gets defensive, there is no way they will be buying anything from you.

Step 2

After complimenting the person for already having what you are selling, explain that it's a common thing for people to buy your product or use your service even if they already own it.

Suppose a potential customer tells you:

"We already have a set of those kitchen knives."

You could respond by saying:

"That's fantastic. I'm glad you see the value of owning a great set of kitchen knives. And because they are so great, many of our clients have found that they make great birthday and holiday gifts. In fact, one of my customers has already bought four sets from me and gives them away as wedding gifts."

Or, suppose you come across a person who already has a regular housecleaning company servicing their home. You might tell them:

"It's great to hear you already use a housecleaning company. There is no question that everybody should have professionals come in and do a deep clean. In fact, our method for deep cleaning is unique to our company, and customers that have been using other companies switch over to us all the time because of our deep-cleaning methods. What we do differently is…"

By letting the person know that switching companies or buying a product they already own is a common practice, they will be more likely to do it. Creating the *bandwagon effect* keeps the conversation professional and won't give the potential customer the impression that you are trying to demean any decisions they've made in the past. You are simply pointing out what others have done.

Step 3

The final technique to convince somebody to buy your product or service, even if they already own or use it, is to recognize similarities and then emphasize differences in what you are selling. First, ask the potential customer what they like the most about the product or service they already own or use and then explain how what you are selling is similar. Although recognizing similarities is important, you should spend the majority of time emphasizing differences. If you spend too much time highlighting similarities, the potential customer won't have justification to make a change—if it ain't broke, don't fix it. But if you respectfully emphasize the differences, they might be swayed enough to make the switch. And the more you know about your competition, the better you will be at pointing out the differences.

Suppose you are selling a cable television subscription and the person you are talking to already subscribes to another provider. Your conversation might go as follows:

Sales Rep: "It's good to hear that you subscribe to a cable service. It's clearly the best option for getting a variety of channels at a low cost. I get a lot of people that switch from their current provider to what I offer because of our pricing and programming options. What do you like most about your current cable provider?"

Customer: "The channels they offer fit the needs of my family, and we get a good price for the number of channels we have access to."

Sales Rep: "And that's what a cable company should offer. In fact, if you stack up our pricing and channel selection with your current company, there aren't many differences. The reason most people switch to our service is because our pay-per-view movies are $2 instead of $5, and also because we give two-hour time windows for service calls. I've spoken with several former customers of your current provider, and they've told me their biggest frustration was waiting around most of the day until the technician arrived. But with us, we give you a specific two-hour time window so you don't have to plan your entire day around the cable company."

Being able to highlight the specific differences in what you offer increases the chances of the potential customer switching to your product or service.

To review, when a potential customer already has what you are selling, you should:

1. Acknowledge their intelligence
2. Explain how common it is for people to switch over
3. Recognize similarities and emphasize differences

These three techniques are effective—unless the potential customer is contractually obligated for a certain amount of products or number of services. If this is the case, the company you represent may offer other programs or discounts to relieve the person from their commitment.

4. They Need It

The fourth and final qualifier takes place when you observe a need for what you are selling. For example, if you were selling a pest control service, a homeowner would qualify before you said a word to them if you noticed spider webs hanging from their home, ant hills in their yard, or wasp nests in their eaves. Or, if you were selling a yard-maintenance service and observed a yard where trees needed to be trimmed and flowerbeds needed weeding, you would certainly want to approach the homeowners.

The need for some products and services is easily identified, but it isn't always so simple. A colleague of mine owned a carpet-cleaning company and then a few years later started a window-washing company. He told me how difficult it was selling a carpet-cleaning service until he was able to get inside of a home and look at the carpet, whereas he could tell from the sidewalk whether the same home needed their windows washed.

When you observe a need, it's necessary to point it out in a nonconfrontational manner so the potential customer doesn't get offended. The particulars of this technique will be detailed in the next chapter.

Qualifying potential customers is simply a matter of knowing who is worth talking to and who isn't. Sales reps must spend their time talking with people who are likely to buy. Therefore, if a person fails to qualify, it's best to move on to the next potential customer because sometimes the grass is actually greener on the other side.

Chapter 8

High Five

Sales reps hear every objection imaginable. Potential customers will say just about anything to get you to leave them alone. I was once knocking doors when a woman answered talking into her telephone. She whispered to me, "I'm on a long-distance call so you'll have to come back later." She became embarrassed and turned bright red as the last word exited her mouth and her phone started ringing.

Appreciating her creative attempt to turn me away, I quickly said, "You must have another call coming in, so I'll come back another time."

Even if you catch somebody pretending to be on a long-distance phone call, always maintain an attitude of courtesy and professionalism. No matter what a potential customer says or does, you should never talk down to them or treat them disrespectfully. Even if they say something completely bizarre, you should act as though it's something you've heard time and time again. If you act surprised or caught off-guard, the potential customer wins—and you lose.

Transitional phrases help you buy time if you aren't sure how to respond to a question or comment. Commonly used transitional phrases include:

"That's a great question."

"I've heard that same concern from a few other neighbors."

"Well, that's exactly why I'm here."

"That's fine. Let me just tell you what I'm doing for your neighbors."

If numerous contacts express the same concern, adjust your initial approach to address the concern from the get-go. For example, suppose you are selling homeowners' insurance, and contacts keep telling you they already have a provider. You could adapt your initial approach to address this concern by saying:

"Hello. I'm Boston with Quality Homeowners' Insurance. I'm sure you already have homeowners' insurance, most of your neighbors do, but that's exactly why I'm here. We are offering…"

When you identify a common concern, there is no reason to wait for the potential customer to bring it up. By originating the concern, you raise your level of credibility because potential customers know you are aware of their needs. Even if you aren't correct in your assumption, your statement will still prove valuable and not affect your conversation negatively.

In all my days as a salesman, I've never sold a single account without a customer expressing at least one concern. Concerns are imminent in sales, so it should come as no surprise when you hear them. Sales reps should never fear when potential customers proclaim their concerns; in fact, they should encourage it. By keeping your initial approach brief, you give potential customers an opportunity to bring up their concerns early in the conversation. And the sooner they state their concerns, the sooner you can resolve them.

Fortunately, the concerns potential customers express will be fairly similar. In fact, there are five concerns you will encounter the majority of time. In the following pages, I've identified these "High Five" concerns—as well as common responses for overcoming them:

1. Can't Afford It

This concern is expressed in every locality. Neither the poorest or wealthiest areas are exempt from their citizens proclaiming they don't have the funds for what you are peddling. No matter the size of the home or make of the vehicle in the driveway, everybody and anybody can declare they don't have the money to pay for your product or service. And the truth is this could actually be the case in any area, which makes overcoming this concern a challenge. Nonetheless, I believe that in most cases, it's the sales rep who fails to build enough value in what they are selling that makes the cost of their product or service seem unjustified.

The price of your product or service should not be revealed until the decision maker is spoken to. Frequently you will encounter a contact who wants to talk with the decision maker before making a purchase. They will ask you to tell them how much your product or service costs so they can pass it on to their significant other. In this scenario, it's best to be as vague as possible and only reveal the price when you are talking to the decision maker.

Sales reps often make the mistake of revealing the price to somebody besides the decision maker in hopes that the person they have spoken to will be able to sell their product or service to the decision maker. Unfortunately, this rarely turns out the way the sales rep had anticipated. Think about it: Mr. Laird gets home from a long day of work, and Mrs. Laird tells him about the great deal a door-to-door salesperson offered them to maintain their yard. Tired and not wanting to do anything but sit on the couch and turn on the baseball game, Mr. Laird replies, "How much is it?"

To which Mrs. Laird reveals, "It costs $140 a month."

Of course, Mrs. Laird isn't much of a salesperson and fails to build the value in the service, which includes mowing, edging, trimming, and weeding. Thus, Mr. Laird responds, "That's too much money. I'll just take care of it on the weekends."

Mrs. Laird is dejected knowing her husband's good intentions rarely come to fruition. It's likely that Mr.

Laird will forget to do yard work until late Sunday and then hurry to mow the lawn just before dark. Regrettably for Mrs. Laird, her husband's lawn-mowing skills are subpar, and the edging, trimming, and weeding get neglected once again.

But before you go blaming Mrs. Laird for her failed attempt to talk her husband into the service, the sales rep is ultimately at fault for failing to make an appointment to talk with Mr. Laird and build the value of the service before revealing the price. A wise sales rep would have explained to Mr. Laird how a detailed mowing, edging, trimming, and weeding would only cost $35 per week and would free up Mr. Laird's weekends to spend more time doing what he wanted to do.

Despite a sales rep's best efforts to build value in their product or service, there will still be circumstances when potential customers tell you they can't afford what you are selling. Therefore, it behooves sales reps to be prepared with effective responses to combat the "Can't Afford It" concern. Here's what I've found to be the most effective ways to address this concern.

As noted earlier, watering down the price by breaking it up into monthly, weekly, or even daily amounts can give the potential customer a different perspective on what they will be spending. For example, if a sales rep was offering a $500 annual pest control contract, she might say:

"So, the initial service will cost just $80, and then the quarterly services we'll do for just $105, so basically this breaks down to just over $40 a month for a guaranteed pest control service. For just over $1.25 per day, you are going to be getting a completely guaranteed, inside and outside, professional pest control service."

Another technique is to explain how being proactive and purchasing the product or service while you are there will actually save the potential customer money in the long-run. Suppose a sales rep is selling a cleaning solution guaranteed to remove stains of all sorts. A proactive approach might go something like this:

"Since I'm here I can offer you this product at a discounted price, and knowing that you'll have use for it in the future, you are actually saving money by purchasing it now at the discount I'm offering. You can certainly order it another time, but you'll end up spending a lot more money for it."

In essence you are telling the potential customer that if they think they don't have the money to pay for the product now, just wait until they really need it and then they'll have to pay more to get it. If you are viewed as somebody trying to save them money, you will be more likely to make sales to those who suggest they don't have any.

These methods of overcoming money concerns will only get you so far, especially with those potential customers who really don't have money to buy what you are selling. And unfortunately, if this is the case, unless you want to pay for the product or service yourself, you aren't going to make the sale.

2. Talk to Spouse

I alluded to this concern in the last section with the example of Mr. and Mrs. Laird but will be explaining in further detail in this section. I've found that most husbands and wives make financial decisions together, which in my opinion is a good thing for a healthy relationship. However, as a sales rep who encounters this scenario several times a day, this concern can become frustrating and time consuming to overcome. Nonetheless, it's important to handle these situations effectively to be able to capitalize on sales opportunities.

Remember, as was noted in the example of Mr. and Mrs. Laird, do whatever you can to conceal the price until both husband and wife are together. In fact, I typically give the spouse I am talking to the opportunity to tell me they would like to talk with their husband or wife before making a decision. To do this, once I have built value in the product or service, I will say:

"I'm sure this is something your husband/wife would also like to be involved in making a decision about, so let me set up a time when I can catch him/

her at home. Should I come back later tonight, or would tomorrow be better?"

Most of the time the husband or wife will comply with this suggestion, but occasionally the person I am talking to is adamant that it's their decision and not their spouse's. If this is the case, I will continue with my presentation and reveal the price. If there are any questions regarding whether I am speaking to the decision maker, I might ask:

"Is this your department or your spouse's department?"

Or I might say:

"Is getting a home security system something you and your spouse have talked about before?"

If answered in the affirmative, I could confidently proceed with the sale and sign up the person without getting their spouse's consent. However, in most cases I would suggest making arrangements to talk with both spouses before making the sale official. Even if one spouse signs up, I will generally make a return appointment to visit the other spouse and make sure they understand what is being purchased. I might even ask the spouse completing the paperwork:

"Will this be something your husband/wife would be opposed to?"

Or I might say:

"I need to make sure you are 100 percent confident in making this purchase. Is there any chance your spouse won't agree to it?"

If I'm not completely confident that I'm signing up the decision maker, I might ask the person to call their spouse to confirm that he or she will approve of the purchase.

It should also be noted that just because one spouse is convinced that what you are selling is desirable does not mean the other spouse will automatically feel the same way. Therefore, if you make a return appointment, you should start with your initial approach and then attempt to qualify the spouse you haven't spoken to. Never assume a spouse is ready to sign up just because their significant other is sold on what you are offering. When talking with the other spouse, use the information you've already gathered to help generate interest. For example, you might say:

"When I was talking to your wife earlier, she mentioned that you guys have talked about getting this type of service in the past..."

Or you could say:

"Your wife mentioned she had been thinking about getting this product because she..."

Communicating that the person's spouse is already on board with buying what you are selling will give you a better chance to convince their other half of its importance.

The spouse situation is a tricky one because no two situations will be the same. It mostly depends on the couple's relationship and past experiences. Just remember to err on the side of caution when revealing the price and/or signing up one spouse without the other's blessing. Talking with both spouses will solidify the sale and increase your retention rate, which means more money in the bank for you.

3. Think About It

This common concern is the most maddening to hear if you've articulated an effective initial approach. If you offer a discount that is exclusive and you give a *time line* for when it expires, yet the person tells you they need time to think about it, they are basically communicating that their decision to buy will be made on their terms, not yours, or that they haven't listened to a word of your initial approach.

Although this concern comes across like fingernails on a chalkboard, what I've learned is that most of the time this statement is a gentle way for the person to let you know they aren't interested in what you are selling. In my experience if you give somebody time to think about it and leave them a business card, that will be the last time you hear from them. Sales, especially of the door-to-door variety, are impulse buys, and if you give time for the potential customer to think about it, they'll likely talk themselves out of buying what you are selling. When a person requests a business card so they can call you when they've had time to think about your offer, you might tell them:

"I didn't bring any cards with me, and this really isn't a call-in discount. Like I said, we're only out in the neighborhood tomorrow and Wednesday, and once we fill the spots the discount will no longer apply in this area. I could give you our phone number, but you'll probably have to pay a higher price for the service if you call in later."

Or you could say:

"You can think about it as long as you'd like, but as I mentioned, we only have two or three more spots I can do for the half price. If these spots are filled by the time you call, then you would have to pay full price."

Although bold, these statements are great for weeding out people who aren't really interested. If communicated confidently, these responses will immediately disclose whether the person has any interest at all in what you are selling. If they have the slightest bit of interest, they might ask you how much your product or service costs, whereas if they have no interest, they might say:

"Well, I'll just take my chances and call back later after I think about it."

Which, being interpreted, means:

"I hate to tell people 'no,' so I'm going to let you down easy and give you a false sense of interest. But please don't come back or try to contact me again because I'm really not interested."

I would much rather have somebody defiantly tell me they aren't interested and slam their door in my face than have a person give me a false sense of hope by saying they might call me later. These people, although cordial, can end up wasting your time if you attempt to contact them in the future because you think they might have interest because they didn't tell you 'no,' when in reality they have as much interest as the person who slammed the door in your face.

Another technique for dealing with potential customers who tell you they need time to think about your offer is to tell them:

"Not a problem. Like I said, I have about two or three spots available, so I'll just come back in twenty or thirty minutes to give you some time to think it over. In fact, here is my cell phone number. If you know sooner than that, give me a call and I'll run right back over."

This response keeps you in control of the conversation by assuming the person will only need twenty or thirty minutes to think about your offer and then make a decision. If the person isn't interested, they will likely respond by saying:

"I need more time than that. Don't worry about coming back later. I'll just call you if I need it."

The concluding response to consider using when people tell you they need more time to think about your offer is to just ask them directly:

"What is it you need to think about?"

Sometimes it's the simplest question that turns out to be the most effective.

4. Do-It-Yourselfers (DIY'ers)

Because of the availability of information on the Internet, being a DIY'er is easier than ever before. Search engines make it possible to learn how to do most anything with just a few clicks of a mouse.

I'm not much of a handyman, so when we had a dripping faucet in our kids' bathroom, I jumped online to look up telephone numbers of the nearest plumbers. As I was searching, I stumbled across a short video on YouTube entitled "How to repair a leaky faucet." After watching the video, I had the information I needed to make the fix myself.

After a quick trip to the hardware store and ten minutes of labor...voila! I had fixed the faucet without having to call in a professional. Knowing my handyman incapability, my wife was gushing over my accomplishment, my kids were cheering me on, and I must admit, a sense of empowerment rushed through my veins. The satisfaction of doing something yourself is incredibly rewarding, which makes selling a service to a DIY'er a tall task…but not an impossible one.

A few points must be addressed in order to have a chance of selling somebody who tells you they are capable of performing the service you are selling. First, acknowledge your appreciation for people tackling the task themselves and then find out specifically what they do. You might ask:

"I'm glad you appreciate how important it is to _____ (keep your lawn fertilized, protect your home against pests, keep up on housecleaning, have clean windows, etc.). What products (or techniques) do you use to _____ (keep your lawn so green, keep from getting pests in your home, keep your home or windows so clean, etc.)?"

Once the person has identified their products and/or techniques, then explain the benefits of using your products and/or techniques as opposed to what they use—without offending the DIY'er. You aren't trying to prove to them that what they are doing doesn't work, only that what you offer is an upgrade. You can do this by spotlighting these benefits:

Effectiveness

If the service you are selling uses products that only certified applicators should apply, the effectiveness of these products versus what is available at the store should be reviewed with the DIY'er.

For example, pest control products that can be purchased by the public are most likely contact kills versus the residual-based products sold to licensed pest-control applicators. Meaning, spray a spider with a contact kill and it dies, but a residual-based product continues working days and even weeks later to kill spiders that come in contact with the product. Also, with everybody having access to over-the-counter pest-control products, their effectiveness can diminish if pests become immune to the products. Generally, products that should only be purchased and applied by professionals are more effective than the alternatives.

Guarantee

Most service companies offer a guarantee of some sort. The guarantee could be service related, where they will return to the customer's home for no charge to offer a retreat. Or, the guarantee could offer the customer their money back for services that don't achieve the desired results.

Suppose you hire a company to fertilize your grass to help it become healthier and greener, and the technician applying the fertilizer accidentally dumps a large quantity of the product on a particular spot, creating a bright yellow burn mark in your lawn. A reputable company would certainly do what it could to repair the damages by sodding the burned area or giving you your money back from the service performed and perhaps future services.

In contrast, if you were applying a store-bought fertilizer and made the same mistake, there is little chance the store you purchased the product from would repair any damages caused by your application of their product. Or, if you brought back a half-used bag of fertilizer and claimed it didn't turn your lawn green or make it healthier, it would be unlikely that the store would give you your money back. DIY'ers should be made aware that they take on much less risk by hiring out services that come with a money-back or service guarantee.

Supplemental

Sales reps should not expect DIY'ers to completely stop servicing or using products they have found to be effective. Encourage potential customers to continue doing what has been working for them but to also use what you are selling as a supplemental product or service.

For example, if you were selling a window-cleaning service and a potential customer was intent on washing their own windows, you could approach the situation by saying:

"Our services will complement what you are already doing and make your windows look even better. You can continue doing what you have been doing, and we will come in just twice a year and thoroughly clean your window screens to ensure that the dust and pollen that accumulates over the year does not increase the likelihood of your windows becoming dirtier when it rains or when water from your sprinklers gets on them..."

Letting the DIY'er know that you are there to complement what they are already doing and are not trying to replace their efforts will help you to create an atmosphere of teamwork and cooperation—an atmosphere that will increase your odds of selling them on using your service in conjunction with what they are already doing.

Time is money

The last benefit you should point out to DIY'ers is that their time is money. Potential customers should realize that the more time they spend doing things that could be done for them, the less time they are able to focus on more important ventures at home, work, or elsewhere.

Brian B. provided the perfect example of how this should be done when he talked a DIY'er into buying his service even though the person had been doing the exact service at his home for over five years. While talking with the potential customer about his successful business career, Brian found out the man was earning approximately $200/hr. As the conversation continued, he also found out the man was spending nearly two hours a week completing the service Brian was offering to do for him.

So Brian explained to the potential customer that he was spending $400 a week of his time, over $1,500 a month, doing a service Brian was offering to do for less than $100 a month. When the man realized his time could be spent more valuably, he hired Brian to do the service.

Even if you've communicated the benefits of using your services (*effectiveness, guarantee, supplemental* and *time is money*), there will still be those who thoroughly enjoy doing their own services. They may have extra time on their hands, do the services to get their mind off of other things, get a great deal of satisfaction in completing a task, or just do it as a hobby. Regardless of their intentions, the reason for their DIY attitude may outweigh any benefits you explain. However, these four benefits will resonate with many DIY'ers and give you more opportunities to sell them your services.

5. No Reason

Sales reps encounter many occasions when their potential customers are reluctant to give a clear reason why they are not interested. People choose to be coy with sales reps because they don't want to spend time talking to them, or they may want to keep their reason for not buying to themselves. Vague responses by potential customers might include:

"I'm not interested."

"Now is not a good time."

"No thanks."

These ambiguous responses make it impossible for sales reps to identify why the person isn't interested in buying their products or services. Therefore, it is pertinent to flush out the real reasons why the person isn't interested. To do this a sales rep could use *win-win statements* or *assume the reason.*

Win-win statements are suggested so that no matter how the statement is answered, the sales rep achieves a desired result. For example, if the potential customer says they aren't interested in having their windows washed, you could say:

"So, who do you use to wash your windows?"

This is a *win-win statement* because if the person tells the sales rep what company washes their windows, the person has admitted their concern, and the sales rep can begin resolving their concern by pointing out differences in the service they are offering. On the other hand, if the person says they don't have anybody washing their windows, the sales rep can eliminate the previously mentioned concern and move on to another *win-win statement,* such as:

"How often do you take care of cleaning your windows?"

The idea is to use *win-win statements* until the potential customer's concern is flushed out.

The other technique to use when dealing with people who don't clearly express their reason for disinterest is to *assume a reason* for them. For example, you might say:

"Are you worried about having to take time to prepare for us?"

"Is this your spouse's department?"

"Are you not going to be home when we are scheduled to be in the area?"

"Do you already have somebody hired to do this for you?"

Making an assumption puts the potential customer in the position of having to accept your declaration or give you their actual reason for not being interested. There is a chance the person will do neither, and if that's the case, continue to make assumptions.

These techniques are excellent for unearthing even the most reclusive concerns. In fact, certain types of people are more apt to respond to specific statements or assumptions. For example, with men, try challenging their machismo by assuming the reason for their not wanting to purchase your product or service by asking:

"Are you worried about the safety of the product?"

"Does it make you nervous knowing that somebody will be at your home doing this for you?"

"Are you a bit frightened at the thought of this product being used around your home?"

These statements should be made with a soft tone so they don't offend. The intent is not to insult but to flush out their actual reason for not wanting to buy. If done effectively, you'll be surprised how many times the truth surfaces when your assumption isn't correct.

With women, make assumptions about the discount you are offering or your credibility as a sales rep. You might ask:

"Are you guys not really into saving money with discounts?"

"Is this something that even with a discount might be too expensive?"

"Do you not trust me?"

"Is it because of something I said?"

Again, the key to proclaiming these assumptions is to state them in a way that won't offend or come across as critical. They should be said in ways that show concern and compassion for the person and their situation. It might take some creativity to find out what gets certain types of people to open up about their concerns, but finding out why they aren't willing to buy is crucial to being successful in sales.

In conclusion, the "High Five" concerns given by potential customers most often are: *No Money, Talk to Spouse, Think About It, DIY'ers,* and *No Reason.* The key to overcoming all these concerns is having a clear understanding of how you will respond in each scenario. If a sales rep is confident in what they will say, they can effectively overcome these concerns and continue to take the potential customer along the path that leads to signing them up.

Chapter 9

Avoiding Contention

You have everything to lose and nothing to gain from being contentious on the doors. As an uninvited visitor, you should always maintain an attitude of courteousness and professionalism—**no matter what**! Contention is a product of cockiness, and confidence is the antithesis of cockiness. A confident sales rep controls the conversation with straightforwardness and honesty. Knowledge and confidence are intertwined: when knowledge is increased, confidence follows. Cockiness, on the other hand, is entangled with arrogance. A cocky sales rep talks down to potential customers by being spiteful and slandering. If you think you are better than the people you are talking to, contention will abound—and your success will be minimized.

I learned this lesson the hard way as a first-year door-to-door sales rep. It was late July, and I had been knocking doors for about three months. Mentally, I was facing the challenges of longer, hotter days and a week of disappointment in terms of my production. I had a negative attitude, and as a result, the people I attempted to sell were becoming less responsive.

Somehow, I managed to sell four accounts in a neighborhood, and my attitude and production started to change for the better. However, this all changed when the neighbor of one of my new customers pushed my patience over the limit. This neighbor accused me of trespassing on his property and threatened to call the police if I didn't leave the neighborhood. I took exception to his accusation and proceeded to argue with him about trespassing laws. Being that my dad had recently retired as the chief of police and spent over twenty-five years in law enforcement, I felt I had a pretty good case to argue. But even if I did, it shouldn't have mattered because our conversation turned for the worse, and the man ended up calling the police.

I made a few snide remarks to the man and proceeded to knock doors until a policeman arrived. We had a lengthy conversation, and even though he knew I wasn't doing anything illegal, he asked me to leave the neighborhood and not come back to avoid further contention. I reluctantly complied with the officer's request, knowing that I had several more doors to knock on the street, and with the four sales I had already made, there certainly would have been more to follow. I was a bit disappointed knowing that my argument had probably cost me some sales. Nevertheless, my consolation prize was winning an argument and proving my point.

But, to my dismay, this incident cost me much more than a few potential sales. I had infuriated this man so much that he went to all of his neighbors to find out who had signed up for the service I was selling. He ended up finding all four of my customers and convincing each one of them to cancel their agreements. As a result, I lost over $500 in commissions. I was devastated. My arrogance and cockiness had cost me big time. At that moment I resolved to never again become contentious with a potential customer. I was going to be courteous and professional no matter what.

Over the years, it has not always been easy to keep my resolution. People can be extremely rude and insensitive if you catch them on a bad day. But I still believe it's best to "live to knock another day" and avoid confrontation at all cost. It takes humility, and having to swallow a bit of pride, but at the end of the day it's worth it. Sales reps must conduct themselves with class and dignity, regardless of the potential customer's attitude toward them, the company they represent, or life in general.

While working as door-to door-salesman for Orkin Pest Control, I occasionally came across homeowners who would rather eat nails then hire Orkin as their pest-control provider. They may have been former customers who had a bad experience with management or a technician, or they may have heard about a friend or family member's bad experience with the company. Regardless, I would have no idea whether these accusations were valid. Nevertheless, I learned that the best way to respond to their grievances was to apologize, explain my position with the company, ask the person if there was anything I could do for them, and then apologize one more time. For example, upon hearing a negative comment about Orkin, I might respond by saying:

"I'm so sorry to hear that your experience (or your family member or friend's experience) was unsatisfactory. I have only been working for Orkin for two years, so I am relatively new. Is there anything you'd like me to pass on to management so we can make sure this kind of thing doesn't happen again? And again, I am so sorry that you had such an awful experience."

Generally, the contact would reply by saying something like:

"It's not your fault. I'm just venting my frustrations on you."

Disarming the person with apologies makes it impossible for the conversation to become heated. It will do you no good to try and defend a mistake...even if a mistake hasn't been made. A disgruntled person wants somebody to acknowledge that they have been wronged and to receive an apology. That much you can do. If the person wants more than that, well, that's out of your hands, but you can gladly take down the person's contact information and pass it on to management.

The following are two common door-to-door scenarios where conflict is likely to transpire unless you take the proper steps to disarm the person and satisfy their desire to vent anger and frustration.

"No Soliciting" Signs

While knocking doors in various cities and states, I've often wondered how successful a door-to-door sales rep would be at selling "No Soliciting" signs, or at least having the signs as an option to sell if a person didn't purchase what was initially offered. The idea would be to sell the person on the idea that buying a sign would help prevent them from having to talk with people like you again.

Because of the time I've spent as a door-to-door salesman, I've never felt it appropriate to have a "No Soliciting" sign on my own home, but my parents have three of them on theirs. One sign is posted on the front door, another is right above the doorbell, and they also have a "No Soliciting" sticker on the window next to their front door. I asked my dad why he went to such great lengths to discourage door-to-door salespeople from knocking on their door. His response? "Because your mom can't say no."

His statement is entirely accurate, by the way. My mom is a sucker for a good deal. In fact, after a long day of shopping, she will proudly walk through the front door with a bevy of bags and boxes and confidently declare to my dad, "Guess how much money I saved us today?"

With that attitude it's no wonder my dad is adamant about "No Soliciting" signs. Come to think of it, maybe three "No Soliciting" signs aren't enough for my parents' home.

While training hundreds of sales reps on the doors, I have found it interesting how intimidated many of them get when approaching homes that have "No Soliciting" signs. Most are so frightened that they avoid knocking the doors of these homes altogether. Frequently a sales rep will turn to me and ask, "Do you normally knock these?"

Knowing what I know about my mom, of course I knock them. I view homes with "No Soliciting" signs as targets. These are the people who have a hard time saying "no," and/or these are the homes that sales reps avoid because of fear and intimidation. Essentially, these are people who rarely get approached by sales reps and have a hard time turning them down...so why wouldn't I want to knock the doors of these homes?

However, my advice to sales reps is to only knock on these doors if they feel comfortable and confident enough to do so. Once I tell them this, most sales reps look relieved to know I don't expect them to contact homeowners with "No Soliciting" signs. Besides, they are too intimidated anyway, and when the person answers the door, the homeowner easily interprets these insecure feelings, making it nearly impossible for the sales reps to sell anything. In these situations, potential customers often call out sales reps, asking, "Don't you see the sign?"

This question typically embarrasses sales reps, who respond by stuttering and stumbling over their words to explain why they knocked on the door despite the sign. Ultimately it discourages them from knocking on any more doors where "No Soliciting" signs are posted.

Funny enough, when I was training sales reps who were reluctant to knock on these doors, they would frequently ask me to do it so I could show them how it was supposed to be done. And of course, I would oblige their request.

The trick to knocking homes with "No Soliciting" signs is, as has been noted before, to approach the potential customer as a messenger, not a solicitor. I have four rules for knocking on doors with "No Soliciting" signs. And if followed, contention can be avoided and sales can be made.

First: Be Busy

When the person comes to the door, you should be engaged in something else besides acknowledging their presence. By being busy the potential customer is more likely to believe you didn't notice their "No Soliciting" sign.

If you carry a binder or some type of planner, you could be taking notes, or if you have a cell phone, you could be wrapping up a phone call. I even know of sales reps who turn their backs to the door and don't turn around to face the person until they first acknowledge the sales rep. Some even act startled when a potential customer starts talking to them. Whatever the case may be, the person should get the impression that you are occupied.

Second: Apologize

Soften your typical initial approach when talking to people with "No Soliciting" signs. It's even encouraged to begin your conversation with an apology. You might say:

"Hello. I'm sorry to bother you. My name is…"

By starting with an apology, you are acknowledging that you might be in a place where you are unwelcomed. An apology eases any tension the person may have about you knocking on their door. In this instance an apology is not a sign of weakness, rather a sign of courteousness.

Third: Name-Drop

Just as you've learned in a normal initial approach, it's critical to drop names of neighbors as you speak with homeowners with "No Soliciting" signs. You might say:

"Hello. Sorry to bother you. I was just talking with the Lambourne family next door and the Stapleys down the street. They wanted me to make sure I let you know what we are doing in the area…"

This initial approach is 100 percent messenger. There is nothing salesy about it; therefore, the "No Soliciting" sign doesn't apply to you.

Fourth: Acknowledge

Even if you have appeared busy, apologized, and name-dropped there is still a chance the person may ask, "Didn't you see my sign?"

If this is the case, it's best to apologize again, admit that you noticed it, and let them know that your intention isn't to sell them anything. You might say:

"I'm sorry again for bothering you. I did see your sign, and I was just dropping by to let you know what we are doing for the Genessy family across the street…"

Following these steps should deflect possible contention from a potential customer, but it's not guaranteed. There is still a chance you will offend somebody, and if that's the case, continue to apologize.

As a reminder, confidence is crucial when approaching "No Soliciting" homes. If the potential customer suspects any hesitation or nervousness on your part, they will likely call you out for being on their doorstep. But no matter whether they have just one or three "No Soliciting" signs, know that the homeowners of these homes are just as likely to be sold as anybody else—and maybe even more likely if they are akin to my mom.

Asked to Leave

If you've spent enough time in door-to-door sales, you will certainly encounter people who are opposed to your knocking doors in their neighborhood, and they will ask you to leave. A smart way to avoid contention in this scenario is to do exactly as you are asked. My motto is:

You can be asked to leave a neighborhood several times, but you can only be kicked out once.

Meaning, if a homeowner asks you to leave their neighborhood, then oblige and return at a different time or day. Upon your return, if another homeowner asks you to leave, then do as you are asked and return at a different time or day yet again. However, if security or the police get involved and ask you to leave, then consider that being officially kicked out of the neighborhood—and you would be wise not to return.

Being approached by neighborhood security or the police can be unnerving. Sometimes it decimates a sales reps' confidence and throws them into a sales funk. I believe every sales rep should get kicked out of a neighborhood as a rite of passage to their becoming a true door-to-door sales rep; however, it would be ideal if this could be avoided entirely. Most of the time, you will get a sense of when a contact is upset and will likely call security or the police. If you get any feeling whatsoever that this could be the case then leave the area immediately.

The following are things people say to sales reps that generally lead to them making a phone call to security or the police once the sales rep has moved on:

"Did you know you're not supposed to be soliciting in this area?"

"It's illegal for you to be knocking in this city."

"Door-to-door sales are not allowed in this neighborhood."

If you have desires to stay in that area, it would be best to respond to these statements by thanking the person for letting you know you aren't supposed to be there and telling them you will be leaving immediately. If you have driven into the area, walk back to your car and drive somewhere else. If you were dropped off, then walk out of the neighborhood while you wait for your ride to pick you up and take you somewhere else.

That being noted, there are instances when a person might ask you to leave the area but is not justified in doing so. There may not be a law or ordinance prohibiting door-to-door sales even though that is what you are being told. I would still follow the same protocol of thanking the person for making you aware of the restrictions and then leaving the neighborhood and returning at another time or day.

Remember: courteousness and professionalism. Don't let your pride get in the way of succumbing to a warning, even if it's inaccurate. It's not worth the possibility of getting kicked out of an area for good.

In the event that a security or police officer approaches you, it's best to be apologetic and congenial. Depending on the city, you could be charged with a fine, ticketed, or even asked to accompany an officer back to the police station for a background check, none of which would be a productive use of your time or money. Thus, do what you are asked to do—and be nice about it.

You can also be proactive and research the soliciting laws of the areas you are assigned to knock. Some cities require a background check and/or fee to receive a solicitor's license, while others may not have any requirements for knocking doors. Whatever the case may be, you should consult with your superiors to determine the best course of action.

I err on the side of caution and strive to avoid contention at all cost. Avoiding conflict takes humility, maturity, and complete control of your emotions. If you feel an unkind remark making its way to your lips, it's best to bite your tongue. Lashing back and inciting conflict may make you feel better initially, but ultimately your actions may cost you future earnings. It's best to take the high road, move to a different area, and "live to knock another day."

Chapter 10

Three Values of Victory

When forming our first company, McKay, my business partner, and I characterized three core principles that we wanted to define our company's culture. After much consideration we came up with our *three values of victory* that we believe helped us to become the largest residential pest-control company in the state of Utah in a matter of five years. We continue to preach these values to our employees in hopes that our successes endure the tests of time. Because our company was primarily built from door-to-door sales, our sales force is particularly trained to adhere to these principles. *Hard work, mental toughness,* and *commitment* are the principles that we believe have made the biggest impact for our success.

1. Hard Work

"I worked and worked and worked, day after day, night after night, dawn to bedtime. I was driven to succeed, and the way I did that was the way I do everything—I overpower problems with work." —Larry H. Miller

I have observed a disturbing trend since I began as a door-to-door sales rep in the late 1990s. In those days, sales reps were primarily focused on improving in areas they could control, such as what time of day they started knocking, how many people they talked to in a day, what time they quit knocking, etc. Sales reps subscribed to the idea that harder work fostered more success. However, I began noticing a shift in attitude about seven years later as sales reps became more focused on things that others had control of, such as an increase in commissions and a reduction in the required hours to knock doors.

When I was a first-year sales rep in 1998, my employer required all sales reps to knock doors for eight hours a day in order to qualify for certain bonuses. Keep in mind, the eight hours was actual knocking time and did not include meetings, drive time, meal breaks, etc. From start to finish, I was working roughly eleven hours a day, six days a week. Back then, that was the life of a door-to-door sales rep.

In contrast, I had a team of sales reps in 2008 try to convince me that they would be just as productive if they only knocked doors from 5:00 p.m. to 9:00 p.m. They claimed they would be fresher and more focused if they just knocked during the times of day when most people were at home. They argued that being in the heat most of the day was wearing them out and limiting their production during the most optimal time of the day to sell. They also claimed that they needed more "me" time to take care of errands, go out to eat, and respond to phone, e-mail, and text messages.

This team of sales reps also pleaded for higher commissions and additional bonuses to "motivate" them to succeed. Ultimately, they wanted to make the same amount of money without having to work as hard to earn it. And, after conversing with other business owners who hired door-to-door sales reps, I realized many sales reps across the nation were making similar requests. A mentality of entitlement was raging in the world of door-to-door sales.

Despite the decline in a desire to work, while conducting hundreds of interviews with hopeful sales reps, most would claim that one of their strongest attributes was being a "hard worker." During the course of an interview, after detailing the grueling schedule of a door-to-door sales rep, I would ask the candidate, "What are the top three qualities you bring to the table that will help you to be successful at this job?"

Surprisingly, over 90 percent would state that "hard work" was one of their top three qualities. Granted, "hard work" is a subjective term. For a kid who grew up working on the family farm, "hard work" might mean something completely different than it does for a kid who grew up in an affluent suburb whose only job was to keep his room clean. Nonetheless, almost every interviewee proclaimed to be a hard worker.

The truth of the matter is sales reps who work the expected hours, and even additional hours, are much more likely to succeed than those who don't. In order to be successful at sales, a sales rep must possess two traits. First is a strong work ethic, and this doesn't mean a self-perceived strong work ethic but an actual strong work ethic. No matter how difficult or discouraging the day, sales reps must at least work the expected hours. It's a fact that if you're not working, you're not selling.

Matt C. and I were selling door to door in Richmond, Virginia, during the summer of 1999. The Old Dominion State's perpetual heat and humidity seemed to suck more life out of us with every passing day. The air conditioning in Matt's car was a welcome relief, but the more time we spent in the car, the less we wanted to get out and knock doors. To motivate us to get our butts out of the car and on the doors, we made a deal that if we heard a song on the radio by the band Sugar Ray, we would immediately get out of the car and start knocking doors. At the time Sugar Ray had several songs on the radio, so it never took very long for one of their songs to come on and get us back on the doors.

The second trait a sales rep must possess to be successful at sales is talent, which is the ability to confidently talk with anybody and influence them into his or her way of thinking. Jared F. was so confident in his ability to sell that he would often approach people to buy what he was selling even if he wasn't working. One evening while he and several other sales reps were at a restaurant, he began a conversation with the waitress that eventually led to him talking about the product that they were all selling. By the time the dessert plates had been cleared, Jared had made an appointment with the waitress to visit her home and introduce the product to her husband. He visited their home the next day and made the sale.

The combination of hard work and talent almost guarantees a sales rep's success. However, success can still be achieved if one of these traits is lacking. Sales reps who work hard are able to cover up a lot of shortcomings in talent and still prove to be capable of making sales— even more sales than sales reps who have talent but are lazy and lack the desire to work. In sales you only make money if you are standing in front of potential customers presenting your sales pitch, and it's the hardworking, talented sales reps who are the most likely to succeed.

While preparing to sell door to door for my first summer, I was convinced that my only competitive advantage over my co-workers would be my ability to outwork them. I figured what I lacked in talent I could make up for by logging more time on the doors. So, I made two specific goals before the summer began. First, I would knock at least one more hour a day than what was required. I resolved to accomplish this goal every morning before the training meeting. Second, I would make two return appointments every evening after dark with people I had spoken to earlier in the day who needed time to think about my offer. This way I could still make sales when it was dark outside and the other sales reps had already clocked out for the day. My dedication to outwork the other sales reps by putting in more time during the mornings and evenings greatly facilitated my overcoming the learning curve and ultimately becoming the top first-year sales rep in the company.

As with anything that's worth doing, a surefire way to improve performance is through practice and repetition. In sales, the harder you work, the more people you talk to, the better your sales pitch becomes and the more sales you make. And there's something existentially rewarding about a hard day's work. When your shirt is soaked with sweat, your crotch burning from the friction of walking several miles, and your hat completely yellow stained from perspiration, you feel whole, you feel worthwhile…you feel alive! That is the essence of success in door-to-door sales.

I came up with a measuring stick for my sales reps to determine whether they were working hard enough to achieve the success they expected of themselves. I called it:

First Out, Last In

Simply put, if a sales rep is the first one on the doors in the morning and the last one in the office at night, then that's a good indication they are working the necessary time it takes to succeed. On the other hand, sales reps who linger after meetings and are the first ones back to the office in the evening will never realize their full capabilities.

I'll never forget the night Glen P. called into the office after 10:30 p.m. from the home of a customer he had just signed up for service. Most of the other sales reps had quit for the day and made their way back to the apartment, but Glen was still out working. It was no wonder that Glen was one of the most successful sales reps that year. His work ethic masked his deficiencies in talent, and as a result, he made himself a lot of money.

Being motivated to be *first out, last in* shows that you are willing to put in the hours, even if it means working extra hours or after hours to reach your goal. Like Glen, you might have a potential customer who wants to make an appointment for later in the evening after everybody else has gone home for the night. And while the other sales reps are sitting on their couches eating ice cream, you could be making a sale. You have control over how hard you work, and you can determine whether keeping that appointment is more important than a bowl of burnt almond fudge.

A hardworking sales rep realizes that there is momentum in sales, and just because a daily goal is reached doesn't mean the day is over. The first sale of the day is the most difficult to secure, and each subsequent sale becomes easier to acquire. Thus, each day should be worked to its full extent to build on any momentum you've gained.

While knocking doors on the Fourth of July in Jacksonville, Florida, I had my best-selling day ever—and it was because I was determined to finish out the day even if it meant cancelling plans to attend a firework show on the beach with my wife. I was on a roll, and each sale was becoming easier and easier to land. I realized that the next day, I would be starting from zero, so I didn't want the day to come to an end. Inevitably it did, but not until I had tallied twelve hours on the doors and twenty-three sales—an industry record! Even though my goal was to only sell eight accounts that day, once things started rolling, I knew it could turn out to be something special... and it was. Thankfully my wife was quick to forgive me, and we ended up watching the last part of the firework show from our car.

I am acknowledged as one of the hardest-working sales reps in the door-to-door industry. I pride myself on having an ever-running motor that helped me to put in more hours than any other sales rep. However, I was humbled while spending eleven days in Kenya, Africa, on a humanitarian trip, when I witnessed a group of women who worked infinitely harder than I ever dreamed of working.

From the minute the morning sky began to glow to the time darkness engulfed any glimmer of light, the Duruma women in Mnyenzeni worked nonstop to sustain life for themselves and their families. Before the sun appeared over the horizon, I witnessed these women walking to the village dam, some walking over three miles, to fill five-gallon buckets of bacteria-laden water that would be used for drinking, cooking, and bathing. Once filled, the buckets, weighing over forty pounds each, were ever so smoothly placed on the crown of their heads with only a small piece of cloth to cushion the weight. With the buckets securely placed on their heads, these petite women would make the trek back to their homes. And although they moved briskly, the buckets stayed firmly on their heads without the use of their hands. Amazingly, not a single drop of water would fall to the ground.

After bringing the water to their homes, the Duruma women would then go to get firewood to be used as fuel for cooking breakfast and for warmth. They would use a wooden-handled hoe to cut kindling and smaller pieces of wood. With their calloused hands, they would tie the wood together in bundles, place them on the tops of their heads, and walk back home yet again to start a fire and prepare a black tea for breakfast.

After getting their children off to school, it was time to care for the livestock. They fed the chickens and took the goats to pasture, gathered eggs and milked the goats, and then accomplished the daily household chores of hand-washing clothing and preparing the evening meal. After a humble dinner of ugali, corn, and chicken, they made a second trip to fetch water before darkness set in. Without electricity, when the skies went dark, the Duruma women were forced to conclude their day.

An eager and healthy door-to-door sales rep who accompanied me on this trip was talked into shadowing a Duruma woman for an entire day to see if he could keep her pace. Despite his best effort, with blisters covering his hands and his muscles twitching from the shock they endured, he called it quits before dinner. Later that evening, the sales rep confessed that he would gladly knock doors all day instead of having to keep the daily schedule of a Duruma woman. How interesting it is that perspective can be altered when hard work equates to survival instead of sales.

I have no doubt that hard work and success go hand in hand. If sales reps truly have a desire to be successful, they will work hard and keep their sights on their goals. And by doing this, their daily sacrifices become easier to accept and endure.

> *"Hard work is the price we must pay for success. I think you can accomplish anything if you're willing to pay the price."* —Vince Lombardi

2. Mental Toughness

"Mental toughness is to physical as four is to one."

—Bobby Knight

Mental toughness is the ability to remain unwavering in your convictions despite what is happening in the world around you, either good or bad. The biggest challenge of staying mentally tough as a door-to-door sales rep is to appear energized and fresh at every single door. Even if the last person you talked to said horrible things about your mom, you have to forget about it and talk to the next person without carrying over any negative feelings from the previous contact. As far as the person in front of you is concerned, you haven't heard "no" the entire day.

As a door-to-door sales rep, you will contact hundreds of potential customers every week and thousands every month, and you only have one opportunity to make a positive first impression on each one of these contacts, thus the importance of giving your best effort at every single door. You never know which contact will turn out to be a sale, and you never know which contact would have been a sale if you had approached them differently.

Success in door-to-door sales is more than just logging physical hours. The mental hours must accompany the physical hours to warrant a concentrated effort.

Suppose a sales rep works ten hours on the doors but is only checked in mentally for five of those hours. The production—or lack thereof—will not be reflective of the physical effort. The point is, if you are out knocking doors anyway, you might as well be in the game mentally, because having your body there but not your mind is senseless.

Before starting as a door-to-door sales rep, I was working at a lock and supply warehouse for a meager hourly wage. The job consisted of receiving and stocking inventory and pulling and shipping orders. There were days when hours seemed to disappear off the clock, but I couldn't remember a single thing that happened during that time. The job was monotonous and mindless.

I worked with five others in the warehouse, and we all got paid the same hourly wage. Regardless of who worked the hardest, our paychecks looked identical on payday. Monday through Friday we punched in, thoughtlessly performed our daily tasks, and punched out. However, this mentality doesn't cut it in sales. You have to be dialed in mentally to thrive. Selling is a thinking person's job.

The best sales reps are mentally sound at every door. They don't let the good times sway them from giving maximum effort. It's easy to become casual in your approach when times are prosperous. Conversely, they don't let the occasional ill-mannered contact throw them off their game either. Like water off a duck's back, the negativity is dismissed and forgotten.

Unfortunately, Rick S. wasn't able to stay mentally strong after a confrontational contact pushed him beyond his limits. Before the incident, Rick was the top-selling first-year sales rep in the company. An exceptionally hard worker who learned sales techniques quickly, he was on pace to have a very lucrative summer, but that all changed after a run-in with a man who woke up on the wrong side of the bed.

Rick had been in a bit of a slump, and his attitude toward the people he was trying to sell was a bit abrasive. He took every "no" personally and carried the weight of each rejection to subsequent doors. Then the blowup ensued.

One of Rick's contacts wasn't in a very good mood, and he threatened to kick Rick off his property. Being that Rick was at the end of his rope, he reciprocated the man's rudeness. Then the man said he was going to call the police. Before the man could turn to go back into his house, Rick threw his own cell phone at the man and said, "Here. Call the police on my phone."

The man caught the phone, threw it right back at Rick, and aggressively approached him. Fortunately, there was no physical altercation, but as Rick walked away from the home, he kicked an ornamental globe in the man's flowerbed, shattering it to pieces. Rick's emotions got the best of him, and as a result he was never the same on the doors.

From that time on, Rick's production slipped tremendously, and several first-year sales reps surpassed his sales total. At each door Rick was fearful of another confrontation ensuing and had lost all of his confidence. Before the incident his weekly average in commissions was nearly $800, but afterward he was struggling to make half of that on a weekly basis. In fact, Rick didn't make $800 in commissions during his last four weeks on the job.

A couple of weeks after this incident, I visited with Rick to see if I could help him regain his mojo as a salesman. My efforts were in vain. He had been affected so severely by this incident that his mental capacity was incapable of repair. He told me, "I have never become confrontational with anybody in my life. But I was so sick and tired of all the rejection that I couldn't take it anymore. I had to vent it out on somebody."

It's certainly not an easy thing to stay mentally tough when door after door and day after day you are being rejected. But you cannot take the rejection personally. They aren't rejecting you, only the product or service you are selling. Sales reps who stay mentally tough are able to endure the eventual sales slumps.

Byron G., a very successful sales rep, kept his mental edge by jogging from door to door. He believed that any pent-up frustrations from rejection could be relieved by physical exertion. He also felt like the shortness of time between doors kept his mind from dwelling on any negative thoughts or experiences he encountered at previous doors.

To stay mentally sharp, Tyson C. stopped wearing a watch while he was working. When he wore a watch, he felt as though the time of day was dictating his schedule, as he would take breaks when his watch showed a particular time, regardless of his production. But when he left his watch at home, his daily goals became the driving force that dictated when he would take a break. He made a daily goal to have at least one sale or one solid return appointment before taking any breaks. If neither of these two things occurred, he continued to work.

One of the most consistent producing sales reps I ever knew was Dave C. He was a sales machine. For him, staying mentally tough was a matter of keeping a regular routine outside of his working hours. He would play the guitar and go to the gym before starting his work day and would end his days by reading for enjoyment. He was a huge spy novel fan who over the course of a few months would read several books. By allowing his mind and body to concentrate on other things besides work, he was able to keep a mental edge while knocking doors.

Rich M. kept mentally focused at every door by earning his water breaks. He would only take a break for water if he made a sale or a potential customer offered him something to drink. He was mentally focused on selling every person standing in front of him so he could earn his break. As a side note, Rich put a small bottle of water and two granola bars in his cargo-pant pockets every day just in case he didn't "earn" time to take a break for water or food. This earned him the nickname Granola Rich.

Michael J. stayed mentally focused in between contacts by reading through his sales training manual and other sales-related books. As he read about sales principles and techniques, he was able to immediately put them into practice. By trying new things and adapting to what was working, he was able to hone in on ways to effectively communicate with potential customers and increase his chances of selling them.

Mental toughness can be accomplished in a variety of ways depending on life experiences and motivating factors. Finding out what helps you to stay mentally strong while on the doors is a critical step to consistent success. Remember: mental toughness is the ability to remain unwavering in your convictions despite what is happening in the world around you, either good or bad.

"Concentration and mental toughness are the margins of victory." —Bill Russell

3. Commitment

"Quit making excuses. What we're really talking about here is commitment. Until you make a commitment to your dream, it's not a commitment at all. It's just another fantasy. And fantasies don't come true because they're not real, we're not committed to them. When we make commitments, they become dreams. And dreams are very real." —Rudy Ruettiger

I never missed a day of school in my life. Seriously. I was on the local news twice, the first time after graduating from high school with perfect attendance and then a second time for continuing my attendance record by never missing a class in college. I must admit, though, I was tardy once in the fourth grade. I'll never forget it. My next-door neighbor was giving me a ride to school one snowy morning, and her car wouldn't start. I arrived twenty minutes late to school. It was the worst day of my life.

My determination to have perfect attendance was an all-out commitment on mine and my parents' part when I was younger. My parents never planned anything that would conflict with my school schedule. Well, almost never. On one occasion I had to fly home by myself from a family trip to Disneyland so I wouldn't miss my first day of high school. But other than that trip, it was my own doings that nearly caused me to miss school on a couple of occasions.

I broke my ankle playing basketball on a school night and had it cast in the emergency room during the early morning hours, just in time for me to make it to first period in junior high school. I'll never forget how severely my ankle was throbbing and how painful it was when my crutches slipped out from under me and I thumped my freshly broken ankle on the ground. Ouch!

During college, the freezing cold mornings of 6:00 a.m. English class during the dead of winter on a campus located just outside the mouth of a canyon brought winds through the quad that literally froze the snot in my nose. I've never felt so cold in my life. Brrr!

My attendance record could be explained by luck, a strong immune system, or just plain stupidity, but the reality is I made a commitment to myself to be in school every day, and I was fearful of letting myself down. I believed that if I let myself down, I would be more prone to letting others down, and that's not the type of person I wanted to be.

Before starting my first year as a door-to-door salesman, the regional manager had every sales rep write down a specific sales number that they would commit to attaining. It was called your "do or die sales number." And of course, knowing me, I took this commitment seriously. After thinking about it for some time, I came up with my number: 442. I had two reasons for selecting 442. First, no rookie sales rep had ever sold over four hundred accounts, and second, I was a huge fan of Ronnie Lott, the starting safety for the San Francisco 49'ers who wore #42. Thus, 442 became my "do or die sales number."

Before the summer began, I knew exactly how many sales I needed to make each month, each day, and even each hour to sell 442 accounts. Others in the industry were quick to tell me that it couldn't be done by a rookie sales rep, but I was absolutely committed, so that's how many accounts I was going to sell. I committed to accept any sacrifices in order to reach 442. During my time knocking doors, I got up early, worked late, and rarely took any breaks. All the sacrifices paid off because at summer's end, I had sold 464 accounts—a new rookie record!

Those who are committed to do what it takes to be successful at door-to-door sales will be successful. It takes a strong inward commitment to do a job that most people won't even consider. It's certainly not a glamorous line of work. Have you ever heard a child say that he or she wants to grow up to be a door-to-door salesperson? Me neither.

I take that back. It did happen on one occasion. I was knocking doors in Cedar Fort, Utah, when a young boy, probably around eight years old, came to the door with his mom. As I attempted to sell the boy's mom, he looked up at her and said, "Mom, I want to do what that man is doing."

To which his mom replied, "Oh, honey, I'm sure this man doesn't love knocking doors. He can't be making that much money, and I bet his wife wishes he did something else."

This made me smile…and I played along, nodding my head in agreement and telling the boy, "Your mom's right. You don't want to be a salesman. You should fly airplanes instead. Pilots get all the girls."

The reality is, the boy's mom was partially accurate in her assumption. I've never loved knocking doors. However, she was mistaken about the amount of money to be made. I believe it's the quickest path to making the most amount of money in the shortest period of time… legally. I have no doubt that door-to-door sales reps earn every penny they make—and some of them make a lot of pennies.

Being undeniably committed means that the devotion and dedication it takes to be successful is consistent on the good days as well as the bad days. It's easy to be committed on the good days, but those who are truly committed remain steadfast on even the most challenging days. Sales reps who quit early when there is still daylight to knock another door or call it a day when things aren't going their way will have difficulty reaching their full potential. If you've made a commitment to an employer, family member, friend, or most importantly to yourself, you owe it to yourself to honor that commitment. Steady sales reps who keep their daily commitments are most likely to succeed.

"There's no abiding success without commitment."

—Tony Robbins

Those who have a desire to be exceptional in sales must be willing to incorporate the *three values of victory* into their day-to-day routine: *hard work, mental toughness,* and *commitment.* These values create the pillars upon which success is built.

Chapter 11

Sales Reps > Politicians

In 2010, a survey conducted by a worldwide management training organization found that the least trusted profession in the United States was politicians. Sales personnel came in second after a longstanding run in the top spot. I would hope that this study isn't an accurate representation of sales personnel, but as for politicians...I'll leave that one alone.

So why do sales reps get such a bad rap? It could be because of past experiences people have had with untrustworthy salespersons. Or maybe it's Hollywood's fault. *Boiler Room*, *Cadillac Man*, and *Wall Street* are just a few movies that depict salesman as money-hungry frauds who say and do anything to make the sale. Whatever the reason, even the most truthful sales rep could be perceived as corrupt because of associated guilt and not from actual evidence.

To this day, my wife and I still don't trust car dealership sales reps because of a bad experience we had nearly twenty years ago. After spending just over two hours with a sales rep answering questions, test driving the vehicle, and negotiating terms, we finally came to an agreement on a purchase price. We were thrilled to be getting the vehicle we wanted for monthly payments that fit within our budget.

The only thing left to do was to sign on the dotted line. The salesman went back to his office to print our paperwork and talk to his manager. Once the paperwork was printed, we were ushered into the manager's office to make it official. As we reviewed the contract, we discovered that the monthly payment price was $18 higher than what we had agreed to. This was frustrating because the salesman knew this payment didn't coincide with our budget. The manager proceeded to tell us that he "had to" add the additional $18 per month to what we had agreed upon because of a "financing fee" the salesman failed to mention. The salesman halfheartedly apologized for his error and told us the additional $18 per month was required for the type of financing we were receiving.

At this point we were clearly agitated, and I told them that if they weren't willing to sell the vehicle for what was originally agreed upon, then we would have to walk away from the pending purchase. The two then proceeded to reprimand us for wasting their time. I couldn't believe what was happening. We were being lied to and condemned for not agreeing to terms we hadn't agreed to in the first place. We left the dealership carless and disgusted with the entire experience.

The next day I called a friend of mine who had worked as a salesman for a car dealership and asked him about this "financing fee." He told me he had never heard of such a fee and suspected the salesman agreed to sell the car to us for too far below the sticker price, and his manager had to find a way to raise the price in order to cover up the salesman's pricing error. My friend commended us for walking away from the sale because in his opinion, the salesman and his manager weren't being honest. Interestingly enough, the car dealership we walked away from went out of business a few years later...something I don't chalk up as coincidence.

Over the years we have bought vehicles from several wonderful sales reps; however, the bad taste in our mouths from our first car-buying experience still lingers. When trust is violated, it takes a long time to forgive and forget. And for some, forgiveness isn't an option no matter how much time has passed. Despite the bridges that can be burned, some sales reps still continue in their dishonest ways. From my experience in door-to-door sales, I have identified three types of sales reps who choose to be dishonest:

1. Dishonesty = Success

Over my years of training hundreds of sales reps, I've witnessed how dishonesty creeps into conversations and over time can spread into every aspect of a sales rep's dialog. Unfortunately, once potential customers believe misleading information and sales are made, sales reps begin to rely on these falsehoods as necessary vernacular to achieving success. As this downward spiral continues, it's only a matter of time until sales reps start accepting their falsehoods as truth, and then it becomes nearly impossible to correct their behavior.

The most unfortunate aspect of this behavior is that sales reps don't realize that if their fabrications were eliminated, they could likely achieve the same results without having to be dishonest. In the end, lies don't sell customers, a sales rep's confidence, knowledge, and passion in what they sell do.

One summer my company employed a sales rep who told a group of people that the pest control service he was selling would guarantee the elimination of box elder bugs in and around their homes. However, he knew the service was incapable of complete elimination because of the box elder trees in the area. Complete control of these pests would have been an impossible undertaking, unless of course the box elder trees were cut down. Nonetheless, he continued to make this declaration because several homeowners were buying the service. In total, he sold seven homeowners on the same street, telling each that the service would completely eliminate box elder bugs.

The moment of truth arrived when the service technician arrived to service the customers' homes and they told the technician what the sales rep had told them about eliminating the box elder bugs. The service technician explained the breeding and swarming habits of the pests and how complete elimination would be impossible without the removal of the box elder trees.

Although most of these accounts ended up cancelling the service because they felt deceived, a few actually continued to receive service. Two of the customers said they didn't believe what the sales rep was saying but figured the service would be worth trying because the sales rep was so passionate about it. Another customer said he knew he was being lied to because he had researched box elder bugs and knew the only sure way to eliminate them was to eliminate the box elder trees. Nevertheless, this customer chose to stay with the service because he figured if his neighbors were doing it, then he should too.

Thus, three of the seven accounts stayed with the service even though they knew the salesman hadn't told them the truth. I would suspect if the sales rep was honest and set a realistic expectation with all seven potential customers, most of them would have signed up for service anyway—and none would have changed their minds once the service technician came to their homes.

Just so I make myself clear:

You do not have to be dishonest to be successful in sales.

2. Money > Ethics

Another reason why sales reps choose to be dishonest is because they love the dollar more than their dignity. I'm not suggesting that making money is evil, but I do believe that "the love of money is the root of all evil," as Paul the Apostle so eloquently wrote to Timothy (1 Tim. 6:10). When money becomes the only motivation, morals go missing.

In my observation, the concepts that sales reps mislead their customers about the most are the length of the service agreement and the guarantee or warranty associated with the product or service they are selling. Lying about the length of the service agreement is more likely to occur if the sales rep gets paid full commissions before their customers complete the required term commitment. For example, if a one-year service agreement is being sold and the company pays full commissions to its sales reps after the customer has received service for six months, some sales reps will mislead their customers into believing that after six months, they can choose whether or not to continue receiving services. This isn't an issue for most sales reps, but there are those whose love of money triggers them to look for ways to take advantage of the system.

Rather than give false information to their customers, sales reps should explain the customer's obligation and expectation of committing to a one-year service agreement as follows:

"We want you to try us for a year so we can prove to you that we are worthy of your business, but our long-term goal is to provide our services at your home as long as you live in it."

By being honest and up-front about service expectations and long-term goals for their home, you will earn more trust and respect from your customers, who will know that you are looking out for them long-term and not just trying to make a quick buck.

Sales reps also deceive their customers by overselling them on the product or service's guarantee or warranty. This is the classic oversell and under-deliver scenario. When their bottom line is on the line, dishonest sales reps will say almost anything to get the sale. When money is the only motivator, *sales prostitutes* and *yes ma'am, no ma'am* sales reps come out in full force, walking the streets with no dignity or self-respect.

Don't get me wrong, money is and always will be a great motivator, but if it's the only motivator, integrity can be compromised and sales reps will say whatever it takes to convince the potential customer that their product or service is something they won't be able to live without.

3. Lack of Knowledge

Sales reps who don't know enough about what they are selling are more likely to be dishonest out of ignorance. Uninformed sales reps commit errors of omission because of their lack of knowledge in the product or service they sell. These errors may be unintentional, but they still have the same effect on potential customers and the company the salesperson represents.

You owe it to yourself, the company you work for, and also to the people you talk with to know as much as you can about the product or service you are selling. As has been noted, work ethic doesn't just take place at the point of sale; it also takes place in your preparation to sell. The more time and effort you put into learning about what you are selling, the more your potential customers will believe what you tell them.

Inevitably, sales reps will be asked questions they don't know how to answer. Instead of trying to make up an answer, it should be understood that potential customers appreciate a sales rep's honesty in admitting their lack of knowledge. If a sales rep gets stumped, rather than changing the subject or answering the question dishonestly, a sales rep could say:

"That's a great question, and I don't know the answer, but if you give me a minute to call my manager, I can have an answer for you shortly."

Comments such as this will be welcomed by potential customers because they demonstrate a concerted effort being made to answer the person's question honestly. A candid confession of ignorance is refreshing to hear and also communicates to the potential customer that the sales rep isn't going to make up answers to future questions.

Suppose a salesperson works for a housecleaning company and is asked if the chemicals used to clean are dangerous for kids or pets. Some sales reps, even if they aren't familiar with the dangers of the chemicals being used, might quickly respond by telling the potential customer they have nothing to worry about. However, a better way to respond would be to say:

"As you know, all chemicals can be dangerous, but the products we use are approved for residential use around kids and pets. I don't know the specifics about all of the products we use, but if you'd like I can get you the MSDS sheets of each product we'll be using in your home."

This answer is straightforward and shows a genuine consideration for the person's concerns. Responses in this vein will help sales reps earn trust and respect from those they are trying to sell. Sales reps give their customers a lot of information during the course of a sale, so it's important they are honest throughout the entire process. The slightest fabrications start to create a web of entanglement that sooner or later can ensnare sales reps and expose them as liars.

I strongly believe that it's just as important to work ethically as it is to have a strong work ethic. Both traits result in sales excellence. Being able to see things from a sales rep's point of view as well as from a business owner's point of view, I can confidently say that deceitful sales reps will ultimately be discovered. It's only a matter of time. Thus, it's better to be truthful and up-front from start to finish. A clear conscience holds more value than money earned by unethical practices. In sales...honesty *is* the best policy.

Chapter 12

Three Deadly Sins of Sales

My most intense period of training was in 2001 and 2002, when I conducted on-the-door training with almost two hundred sales reps in a period of six months. During that time, I knocked doors as far west as Santa Rosa, California, as far east as Virginia Beach, Virginia, as far north as Chicago, Illinois, and as far south as Ft. Lauderdale, Florida. Besides racking up some serious airline rewards, I also witnessed three reoccurring tendencies that were hindering sales reps' production. While observing sales reps in action, I noticed that every single one was guilty of committing at least one of the *three deadly sins of sales*— and most sales reps were committing two or all three of them.

Fortunately, with proper training and practice, these sins can be absolved once they have been identified. Identification is the first step to recognizing a problem; therefore, each of the *three deadly sins of sales* will be identified, and then a *How to Fix It* section will follow, sharing advice and examples of how each sin can be overcome.

Sin 1 The Robot

If the definition of insanity is doing the same thing over and over and expecting different results, then most sales reps are downright crazy. In my observation, door-to-door sales reps who struggle with consistent production almost always repeat the same words and phrases during the sales process, despite their ineffectiveness. These sales reps somehow believe that something is wrong with entire neighborhoods or cities of people because their words don't seem to resonate with potential customers, when in fact it's the sales reps' lack of originality and creativity that creates a chasm between them and their prospects. Repetitious jargon is a lazy and impersonal way to communicate that ultimately leads to people feeling as though they are listening to a canned script rather than having a genuine discussion.

This sin manifests itself during the entire sales process but especially during the initial approach. Many sales reps repeat those precious forty-five seconds or so that are vital in establishing credibility verbatim at door after door after door. If this is the case, the sales rep might as well be replaced with a recorded message. Potential customers deserve to feel as though what is being communicated to them is fresh, new, and something the sales rep is passionate about.

Unfortunately, this isn't an easy undertaking. Human nature pushes us toward familiar routines. We train ourselves to eat specific foods for certain meals, wake up and go to bed at specific times of the day, and even answer common questions the same ways. For example, until recently, when somebody asked me, "How are you doing?"

I would routinely respond with, "Good. How are you?"

However, a friend of mine informed me that this response is grammatically incorrect and suitable responses to the question should be, "I am well," or, "I'm doing fine."

To get out of my routine of answering this question incorrectly was no simple task. In fact, it took me several weeks to quit responding with, "Good. How are you?"

My children have also developed built-in responses to certain questions. When I talked with my kids after they had come home from school, I would typically ask them, "How was school today?"

Each of them would respond by saying, "Good."

(I'll have to check with my friend to see if that's a grammatically correct response to my question.)

So, to change things up, I decided to adjust my question to elicit more conversation from them and began asking, "What did you like the most about school today?"

Funny enough, they would respond by saying, "Good."

In fact, it took my six-year-old over a month to get out of the habit of answering my new question with his routine response of "Good."

In sales, routine comments and responses to questions can be dangerous because potential customers' needs and circumstances vary. However, sales reps commonly trudge through the same vernacular and somehow expect different results, thinking the people they are talking to need to change, not them. Of course, this attitude will never result in effectively selling anything. Potential customers are too clever not to spot a sales rep who is communicating on autopilot. Sales reps robotically going through their checklist of must say's and neglecting the individual needs of those they talk to commit *sin 1 the robot.*

How to Fix It

There are several ways to fix being a robot. One way is to use the time in between each sales opportunity to self-critique and identify ways to improve. Selling is a thinking person's game, and valuable lessons can be learned after every contact if the sales rep takes time to review their previous conversations and make adjustments as they identify weaknesses.

Another way to avoid sounding robotic is to constantly change your initial approach. While selling door to door, my first goal of the day was to have a unique conversation with every person I met. Of course, I would also set sales and monetary goals, but initially my goal was to never duplicate an initial approach—which isn't an easy thing to do when talking with seventy-five-plus people in a given day. It forced me to think about each door approach, which in turn prohibited me from being repetitious in my conversations. It also kept my contacts attentive because I came across as spontaneous and genuine and not as though I was repeating a scripted sales pitch.

There are a couple of surefire ways to keep each initial approach unique, the first being *name-dropping*, which has already been described in detail, and the second being *catering*, which I will define in the following pages.

When I think about an event being catered, I'm reminded of the first experience I had attending a catered event. I was fourteen years old, and my mom had talked me into attending the wedding reception of one of her clients' daughters. My mom was and still is a great salesperson. And in this case, she not only got me to go with her to the reception, she also talked me into letting her select my wardrobe for the evening. I will never forget being dressed in a black button-up shirt with white pinstripes accompanied by a solid white tie and black slacks. I despised the outfit and thought I looked ridiculous, but I love my mom, so I submitted to her request.

Upon arriving at the enormous home where the reception took place, I felt extremely self-conscious about my clothing. However, those thoughts were quickly forgotten as I entered the world of catered events. Once my mom and I were ushered into the backyard, a man with a tray of hors d'oeuvres immediately approached us, and to my delight there were several more waiters offering tantalizing delicacies on shiny silver trays. And just when I thought it couldn't get any better, soon we were shown to our seats and served a light meal, followed by dessert. As we were leaving, we were given a small bag of goodies. Despite my reluctance to attend the reception, it didn't take long for me to forget about my outfit and enjoy the royal treatment of this catered reception.

As I've had the opportunity to attend several more catered events, I still appreciate how significant these occasions make their guests feel. Being catered to gives people the feeling of importance, which is an innate human desire.

So how does catering apply to sales? Think about it: if your product or service can be catered to the potential customer's circumstances, needs, and/or wants, then you make them feel like an MVP and the sale becomes simplified. The following are examples of how initial approaches can be catered.

Age of the Home

If the product or service makes improvements to the person's home, then catering to the age of their home is a great way to make each conversation unique. Once I have identified how old the person's home is, I can easily adjust my initial approach to each contact. I classify ages of houses into these categories:

- New home (0-5 years old)
- Aged home (6-15 years old)
- Older home (16+ years old)

New homeowners are most likely to buy products and services that will benefit their newest and possibly most important investment: their house. Being that the house is new, the potential customer may not think they have an immediate need for your product or service. Thus, you should focus on what the person can expect to happen as their home ages. For example, a homeowner of a new home may not have any immediate pest issues, but if you explain how over time, as the home settles and cracks and crevices develop along the foundation, pests discover these areas and use them to traffic inside the home, the person may see the value of having a pest control service for preventative reasons.

A new homeowner may not think they need a home security system, but if you explain how thieves target new homes because they are less likely to have a security system, the homeowner might see the value of getting a system installed. Or, if the homeowners are moving into a home that was previously occupied, you could explain how the previous owners could have been targeted for burglary because the home lacked a security system, so it might be the perfect time for them to purchase a system.

Sales reps should realize that selling a product or service to a new homeowner will not likely occur because of an immediate need, so the focus should be on precautionary measures that the product or service will offer when the need arises.

When dealing with potential customers in aged homes, it's important to find out about the history of the home. Ask how many times the home has been sold and whether the current residents knew the previous residents. If they didn't know them, several points can be made when selling a product or service to the current homeowners, such as the cleanliness of the previous owners, whether they kept up on home repairs, and whether they subscribed to the services being offered. A sales rep selling a cleaning service might approach a person living in an aged home by saying:

"I'm sure the previous homeowners cared about the home, but it would be difficult to know whether they ever hired a professional housecleaning service to thoroughly clean it. And not knowing whether their cleaning standards were on par with your standards, now would be a great time to deep clean your home, especially being that we are offering a discount..."

If the current residents have been the only ones to live in an aged home, there is a good chance they have either considered purchasing or have purchased what you are selling. If this is the case, a sales rep should address both possibilities. A home security sales rep might say:

"Being that your family has lived in the home for about ten years, I'm sure you've either thought about purchasing a home security system or maybe at one point actually did. And as I'm sure you are aware, homes this age can be targeted by thieves due to the old style of door and window locks that can be easily picked."

The key to selling in aged homes is finding out how long the current residents have lived in the home, how many other families have occupied the home, and whether the current owners knew the previous residents. Once you know these things, you can cater the product or service to fit the needs of the potential customer.

When dealing with older homes, you should know the same information listed in the previous paragraph. And if you find out the current residents have lived in the home for the entire sixteen-plus years then they should be treated as the experts of their residence. It's likely these residents have had or currently have your product or service. That being the case, you will have to point out how your product or service is an upgrade from what they have used in the past. But remember: these people know much more about their home and its needs than you do; therefore, it's a good idea to ask questions, listen, and talk less than you normally would.

Being that older homes are more susceptible to repairs and/or upgrades, if your products or services can assist their home in this way then the potential customer may automatically qualify for your time. For example: if you represented a roofing company, you might approach the residents of an older home by saying:

"Since you've been in your home for as long as you have, I know you realize how important it is to get your roof re-shingled before it starts leaking and costing you hundreds if not thousands of dollars in repairs…"

The biggest challenge with selling in older homes is that most of these homeowners believe in the saying "If it ain't broke, don't fix it."

Therefore, if they don't have an immediate need for your product or service, they probably won't purchase it. On the other hand, if what you are selling is something they have considered purchasing in the past, they may just decide to go for it since you are there offering it to them for a discount.

How the Home Was Built

Another way to cater the initial approach is to talk about the materials that were used to build the home as it relates to what you are selling. As noted regarding the age of the home, for this to make sense, the product or service must assist in improving the home.

Suppose you are selling a power-washing service. You could approach a homeowner by saying:

"These vinyl homes are recommended to be power-washed every five years to help them look like new again. Our services are guaranteed to..."

Or suppose you are selling a pest-control service. You might say:

"These brick homes become somewhat susceptible to spiders as they nest in the weep holes of the brick. To prevent them from getting inside..."

When applicable, the materials used to build houses can help to differentiate your initial approaches and keep conversations fresh. If the sales rep explains how their product or service specifically benefits the potential customer's home, they will be more inclined to listen and possibly purchase what is being sold.

Unique Features

Sometimes homes have features, such as swimming pools, sandboxes, basketball courts, outdoor fireplaces, or children's play sets. If this is the case, try to explain how your product or service will directly benefit the features of the home.

For example: if you were selling a yard-maintenance service, you might say:

"As we edge around your yard, we will be sure to keep a crisp line around your basketball court and sandbox areas."

If fertilization is also part of the service, you might continue by saying:

"And as we fertilize, we will be particularly careful to keep our products from getting into your fishing pond and waterfall feature."

Observing unique features of homes sometimes takes keen awareness and good observation. I was knocking doors with Tony H. in Springdale, Arkansas, when he mentioned to a potential customer that they didn't have to worry about our pest-control products getting into their swimming pool in the backyard. Tony's statement caught me off guard because I had no idea there was a swimming pool in the backyard. As we left the home, I asked him how he knew they had a swimming pool. He told me that as the potential customer opened the front door, he could smell chlorine and also noticed several wet swimming suits and towels hanging on the bannister inside the home. His quick observations allowed him to cater his approach and personalize the service.

Common Concerns

I explored this topic earlier, but it is worth bringing up again under the context of making each initial approach different. An alert sales rep will identify common concerns from other contacts in an area and then address these concerns in their initial approach, rather than wait for potential customers to bring them up. By identifying common concerns, sales reps are able to make adjustments to their initial approaches in order to make them unique.

For example, if you were selling a lawn-aeration service and several people had mentioned they had the service done last year, you might begin your initial approach by saying:

"Hello. My name is Christy, and I'm with Healthy Lawn Services. We are offering an aeration service for a discount today and tomorrow. I realize you may have had your lawn aerated last year like some of your neighbors, but it's recommended to aerate on an annual basis because…"

Whatever the common concerns, it's simple to address them in an initial approach if sales reps are paying attention to why previous contacts aren't buying from them.

Surrounding Area

In some neighborhoods, houses are in close proximity to one another, whereas others have acres separating them from their nearest neighbors. Some areas seem surrounded by the hustle and bustle of construction and/or land development while others are surrounded by the serenity of streams, ponds, and woodlands. No matter what the differences are in the surrounding areas, a sales rep's initial approach should be customized to educate people as to how their product or service can benefit that person's home based on its surroundings.

For example: if you were selling a home security system in an area with a lot of construction taking place, you might want to include in your initial approach:

"Homeowners in areas like this, where a lot of construction is going on, are extremely vulnerable to break-ins because so many strangers are in the area and able to observe when homes are typically unoccupied."

Or if you were selling pest control in a heavily wooded area, you might say:

"Being that you guys live in an area with a lot of trees, the flea and tick population is much higher than in most areas, thus the need to have a pest-control service."

It takes awareness and creativity to effectively cater your initial approach to potential customers' surrounding areas, but if done properly, it will improve your chances of validating why your product or service is beneficial for them to purchase.

Kids and Pets

People love their kids…most of the time. And let's be honest, some people even love their pets more than their kids. Therefore, if you can bring kids or pets into your initial approach of explaining why your product or service should be important to the potential customer, you will give yourself a good chance of qualifying the person and explaining in more detail what you are offering.

It's easy to detect whether a homeowner has kids and/or pets. You just have to know what you're looking for. You can make educated guesses if you observe toys in the yard, garage, or home; food and water dishes inside or outside; or animal feces on the lawn. Once you've made an observation, you might consider asking potential customers about their kids and/or pets to help them feel more comfortable with your being there. You could say:

"I noticed the dog leash on your lawn. What kind of dog do you have?"

To talk more specifically about what you are selling and how it benefits families with kids, you might consider saying something like this if you were selling a cable television service:

"Something a lot of your neighbors with young kids have liked is that our service offers sixteen channels of 24/7 children's television programs. Our parental control options are also fantastic…"

If you were selling yard maintenance that included weeding, you might say:

"People with pets, like you, really like that our weed killer is organically based and nontoxic for dogs and cats."

It's not difficult to give a unique initial approach to every person you attempt to sell—if you are observant and cognizant of your surroundings. Trying to make each approach different will keep your mind active and your approaches fresh. Each contact should feel as though what you are offering is catered to them specifically and something you are enthusiastic about.

Catering does not begin and end with the initial approach. You must continue to cater the conversation throughout the entire sales process so the potential customer believes the product or service you are offering is a perfect fit for them.

Ultimately, fixing *sin 1 the robot* is about learning how to have conversations with people. When a potential customer opens the door, you don't want them to think they are hearing a rehearsed pitch you've been using all day. Although this might be true, this is the first and possibly only time you will be explaining the service to that particular person, so it must come across as unique and impromptu. Remember: everybody loves a well-catered event, so the better catered your message, the more likely the sale.

Sin 2 Dead Ears

It's been said that we have two ears and one mouth, so we should listen twice as much as we speak. However, from my training experiences, I've observed that most sales reps are more interested in what's coming out of their own mouths than what's coming out of the mouths of the people they are trying to sell.

It's unfortunate how many times potential customers give subtle clues that sales reps completely miss because they are too focused on thinking about what they want to say next—and it's these subtle clues people give that make it possible to personalize the message and increase the probability of making sales. Interesting enough, sales reps who commit *sin 1 the robot* are also likely to commit *sin 2 dead ears* because they are so intent on saying what they routinely say that they fail to give ear to what the potential customer is saying back to them.

During my first year as a door-to-door salesman, I had an experience with my sales manager and good friend Matt C. that proved to be the turning point for me to focus more on listening to potential customers. As Matt was observing me on the doors in Bessemer, Alabama, we came upon a man who told us he wouldn't need our services because he serviced his own home. During the course of our conversation, he stated:

"I'm just taking advantage of having more time to get things done around the house."

Although I thought nothing of this comment and continued with my explanation of the benefits of our service, Matt picked up on the clue and asked him:

"Do you have more time around the house because your job situation has changed, or are you on vacation?"

Matt nailed it. The man had recently lost his job but was reluctant to divulge that information to us and only did so because of Matt's question. Thanks to Matt we were able to move on to the next door much quicker knowing the man wouldn't be able to afford our service in his present situation. If Matt hadn't asked the question, I might have wasted time trying to sell something to somebody who couldn't afford it and had plenty of extra time to do it himself.

A few years later, in Kansas City, Missouri, I encountered a similar experience while training a new sales rep, Bob. G. I was observing Bob as he engaged in a conversation with a potential customer who was giving all the appropriate verbal and nonverbal clues of wanting the service. She was mirroring Bob's body language, agreeing with everything he was saying, and even told him that she wanted the service. However, Bob was so intent on finishing his canned pitch that he carried on for several minutes before finally asking her if she wanted to schedule a time for the service. To which she replied, "It's about time you asked me. I've been trying to tell you I wanted to sign up for the last five minutes!"

A valuable lesson on the importance of listening can be learned from both experiences. On one hand, Bob was wasting time with somebody who was ready to purchase the service, and on the other hand, I was wasting time with somebody who wouldn't have purchased the service. In both cases, we squandered time—time we could've spent making more sales.

To be an effective salesperson, you must learn to pay attention to the verbal clues potential customers communicate. Sales reps who commit *sin 2 dead ears* become so fixated on what they want to say that they miss out on clues that would help them determine whether or not to proceed with their conversations.

How to Fix It

The best way to avoid *sin 2 dead ears* is to practice the technique of *stop, drop, and ask.* When a potential customer begins talking, you must immediately *stop* whatever you are saying, even if you are in midsentence.

Almost daily I take part in or observe conversations where two people are talking over each other in an effort to finish a thought. It becomes a race to see who can finish their sentence first, and what happens is neither person hears what the other is saying. That's what I call an epic failure to communicate. Thus, when a person starts talking over you, *stop* what you are saying and listen to what is being said because they aren't listening to what you are telling them anyway.

Second, *drop* whatever it is you think you were going to say next. Don't worry about finishing the sentence you were cut off from completing. Instead focus on what the potential customer is saying even if it doesn't relate to what you were trying to communicate. Most of the time people stay on track with what is being said, but sometimes they ask a question or make a completely random, unrelated comment. Either way, *drop* whatever you were planning on saying.

Finally, you should *ask* at least one follow-up question that relates to the person's comment or question. If the potential customer goes off on a tangent about their grandkids and you were just about to explain the price of the product, place this thought on the back burner and *ask* a question or two about their grandkids. Being willing to *ask* questions that relate to what's on your potential customer's mind will help you to gain their respect, and in turn they will be more likely to ask you questions that relate to items you discuss.

Once you have effectively used the technique of *stop, drop, and ask*, it's important to get the conversation back on the track of leading the person toward a purchase. To assist you in this effort, use a transitional phrase, such as:

"And like I was saying, the price of the product..."

If the potential customer makes a comment or asks a question that is relevant to what you are selling, then you should ask several follow-up questions related to what they have said. For example, if you are selling a pest-control service and the person asks:

"Do you take care of spiders?"

You should answer this question with questions of your own, such as:

"Where have you noticed spiders?"

"Have you noticed several or just a few?"

"Are the spiders more black or brown in color?"

"Are you seeing them upstairs, downstairs, or both?"

"When do you notice them the most? In the morning, afternoon, or evening?"

This technique, called *shotgun questioning*, is designed to help potential customers build value in your product or service. In this example, the questions should prompt the potential customer into recalling all the instances when they noticed spiders; thus, they are building value in the service themselves, without the sales rep having to do it. When using this technique of questioning, it's important to ask each question thoughtfully and not in a manner that makes the person feel as though they are being interrogated.

In the previous example, when explaining the details of the pest-control service, it's important to focus the explanation on how the service protects the home from spiders—not ants, wasps, crickets, or any other pest—just spiders. By customizing the service explanation to fit the customer's needs, the sales rep is much more likely to keep the person's attention and ultimately make the sale.

Then, if later in the conversation the potential customer asks:

"What about ants? What do you do for them?"

The sales rep should begin another series of *shotgun questions*:

"Where have you noticed the ants?"

"What color are the ants?"

"Are you seeing them inside or just outside?"

Actively listening to what potential customers are communicating is a learnable skill that shows that you have interest in the person you are talking to and you aren't just there to present a scripted speech you've shared with the rest of the neighborhood. Make it a habit to *stop, drop, and ask* when a potential customer is speaking. By doing so you will show respect and concern that will likely be reciprocated, making the sales process much more streamlined and simplified.

Sin 3 Know-It-All

> *Mr. Know It All*
> *Well ya think you know it all*
> *But ya don't know a thing at all*
> *Ain't it, ain't it something y'all*
>
> —Kelly Clarkson, *Mr. Know It All*

It's impossible to know everything there is to know about sales. Nevertheless, some sales reps think they've got it all figured out. While observing hundreds of sales reps in action, those who think they know it all are challenged with producing sales on a consistent basis and being able to make the necessary adjustments to improve. In other words: if you think you know it all, you will never get better.

In 2010, Chuck S. was one of our most promising new sales reps. His successful college baseball career and accomplishments in a previous sales jobs proved he was willing to work hard and had the experience to be a fantastic door-to-door sales rep. I figured he would be a shoo-in for top rookie sales rep in the company. And after his first two weeks on the job, my assumption was confirmed as his eighteen accounts led every other sales rep in his office, including his experienced sales manager, who was the top rookie sales rep the previous year. However, during the next twelve weeks, Chuck only managed to sell twenty-eight more accounts. His weekly sales totals from his final twelve weeks were five, four, four, one, four, four, one, three, zero, zero, one, and one.

Chuck's managers spent several hours with him trying to figure out what was causing his ongoing slump. I also knocked doors with him on a couple of occasions to see if I could offer any assistance in the matter. Despite our efforts, the mystery of Chuck's sales plummet continued until his branch manager finally figured out what was wrong. While having a conversation with his manager, Chuck proclaimed, "I'm doing exactly what Lenny does, but it doesn't work in this city. So if it's not me, then something has to be wrong with the area you have been sending me to work."

The branch manager responded to Chuck's comment by saying, "So you're telling me that you are doing exactly what it has taken Lenny years to perfect, and that somehow you have figured it all out in less than a month?"

Chuck wasn't about to backtrack on his statement and continued to argue that he had learned everything there was to know about selling door to door and that it was not his fault his production was rapidly declining. The next day, the branch manager spent an hour knocking doors with Chuck and observed him fumbling over his words and giving up way too early with potential customers who were qualifying for more time. After he'd seen enough, the branch manager knocked a few doors with Chuck and made a sale within fifteen minutes, thus proving that the area had nothing to do with his failure to flourish, but it was Chuck who was ultimately responsible for his own demise.

Chuck's arrogance and *know-it-all* attitude had blinded his perception of reality, and he proved Kelly Clarkson's lyrics correct: "Well ya think ya know it all. But ya don't know a thing at all."

A *know-it-all* attitude prohibits progress and poisons production. The skills to be successful in sales are mercurial, and even though patterns in human behavior can assist in making educated decisions on what to say and when to say it, there has never been a sales tactic proven to work 100 percent of the time. Sales reps who propose to *know it all* are their own worst enemy and will never reach their full potential.

How to Fix It

I have never watched an episode of *Seinfeld* from start to finish, which presumably makes me one of a very select group of adults who can claim such a thing. But I don't tout this to boast; in fact, I wish I knew more about the iconic sitcom because of the countless times in my life that I've heard, "You know, just like that *Seinfeld* episode when…" and I don't have a clue what they are talking about.

Nonetheless, I have only regretted not watching the television series once in my life: May 14, 1998. It was during this Thursday evening that the 179th and 180th episodes aired: the final two episodes of the series.

Not being a fan of the show and unaware that an estimated 76 million viewers were tuned in, I went about my evening routine of knocking doors. However, for the sixty minutes or so that the show was airing, I wasn't sure if a single household in Homewood, Alabama, wasn't watching the finale because few homeowners answered their doors, and those who did treated me as a pariah.

It was at that moment I wished I had been a fan of *Seinfeld* because I was sure I would have been able to join a potential customer who was watching the show, build on the common love of *Seinfeld*, and then, once the show was over, explain what I was selling and walk out of the house with a signed service agreement. But instead, I struggled the entire evening and didn't make a single sale.

The point is, I have never thought I knew all there is to know about sales—or iconic sitcoms for that matter. Whenever I have failed, I have only looked inward to resolve my inadequacies. *Know-it-alls* don't look inward when the going gets tough, they find somebody or something else to blame. Fixing the problem of being a *know-it-all* starts with accepting your own failures and realizing that learning about sales is an ongoing process that will never be completely understood. Being open minded to continual learning is a sure way to realize steady improvements.

While conducting training meetings, I could easily point out the sales reps who were going to be the quickest learners. They were the ones who would frantically write down everything I said and ask numerous questions about each subject being taught. It was obvious they had a passionate desire to learn and be successful, and this desire translated on the doors as well. While knocking doors with sales reps in a training environment, I appreciated those who would take notes while I was talking with potential customers and ask questions as we walked from house to house. I knew these sales reps would likely achieve their goals.

I made a habit of keeping notes while observing sales reps in action. I continued this practice with every sales rep I trained for two specific reasons. First, I wrote down observations that would allow me to give each sales rep specific feedback on ways he or she could improve. And second, I would write down words, phrases, or other things a sales rep said or did that I felt was an improvement to what I said or did—even if it was a sales rep on the job for their first day. I tried to learn something from everybody I had the opportunity to observe.

Before publishing this book, Griffith J. was one of the last sales reps I observed knocking doors, and he taught me something I hadn't thought of in my many years as a door-to-door salesman. While knocking in Woodbury, Minnesota, Griffith was explaining the benefits of a pest-control service that offered wall dusting in the winter. The potential customer didn't think the wall dusting would be effective for their home because it had blown-in insulation when it was constructed. I had heard this concern many times but had never figured out an effective way to address it. To my surprise, Griffith proceeded without hesitation and confidently explained:

"As you know, blown-in insulation condenses over time, which leaves gaps in your wall voids that pests eventually use to build their nests and reproduce. Over time, these gaps in the insulation can house hundreds of pests, making the wall-dusting service one of the most important services we can provide for your home…"

Genius! And to think, after all those years of knocking doors, I had never thought of answering the blown-in insulation question that way. It made sense to me, and more importantly, it made sense to the potential customer.

Sales reps must be teachable to prevent them from thinking they know everything. Being willing to accept criticism is another way to keep learning and making improvements, and sales reps should never take offense when they are being critiqued. I've learned that even the most inexperienced sales reps are capable of teaching me something that can help me to improve.

Another technique that helps prevent sales reps from becoming *know-it-alls* is teaching them how to make the potential customers they are talking to the *know-it-alls*. This is done by using acknowledging pre-statements before stating facts. Effective acknowledging pre-statements include:

"As you know…"

"I'm sure you already know…"

"I know that you are familiar with…"

To achieve their full effect, these acknowledging pre-statements should be accompanied by a head nod.

If communicated correctly, acknowledging pre-statements give the potential customer a feeling of empowerment, when in reality they may not have a clue about what you are telling them. But more important than the potential customer's feeling of empowerment is the fact that they are accepting the sales rep's information as truth.

Just as important and effective as an acknowledging pre-statement is an acknowledging post-question, such as:

"Right?"

"You understand?"

"Does that make sense?"

These questions should also be asked with a head nod to get the potential customer to agree with what you just told them. If both of these techniques are used correctly, the potential customer will feel as though they are in control of the conversation—when in reality, you are pulling all the strings.

The following are two examples of how to effectively use an acknowledging pre-statement and acknowledging post-question. While selling a pest-control service, you might say:

"I'm sure you already know that ant colonies spread if you spray their trails (nodding your head up and down). The ants leave a pheromone behind, and that's how they follow each other, and if they can't locate the pheromone trail, the ants that can't find their way back to the colony will start another colony. It's called budding, and of course you wouldn't want that to happen (shaking your head back and forth), right?"

In this example, the sales rep doesn't come across as a *know-it-all* because the information is given as though the potential customer already knows it. And by ending the statement with an acknowledging post-question, the sales rep leaves the person with almost no choice but to agree with what the sales rep has told them.

While selling a window-cleaning service, you might say:

"I know that you're familiar with how difficult it is to clean hard-water stains (nodding your head up and down), so that's why your windows with these stains will be charged a bit more. But keep in mind, we will also be coating these windows to make it more difficult for hard-water spots to develop in the future, which I'm sure you'd like to make sure happens (nodding your head up and down). Does that make sense?"

It's interesting how making the potential customer the *know-it-all* is an effective technique, but when a sales rep comes across as a *know-it-all* it's considered a deadly sin. It just goes to show how fine a line there is between success and failure in sales.

In summary, all *three deadly sins of sales* can be corrected no matter how engulfed a sales rep is in one, two, or all three of them. As sales reps become able to make each conversation unique, listen to what is being said to them, and always look for ways to improve, their sales skills will increase—along with the dollars in their wallet.

Conclusion

So, there you have it. Making sales is that easy. Well, not really. The truth is, successfully selling products or services is a multifaceted skill that can only be learned with dedicated desire and persistent practice. And similar to the development of any skill, a learning curve must be overcome before success is realized. Door-to-door sales in particular require adequate time on the doors, interacting with potential customers to accomplish learning curve dominance.

Inexperienced door-to-door sales reps need about two weeks to begin feeling comfortable with their initial approach. This two-week period also gives sales reps a good sample size of what concerns potential customers will reveal to them. Thus, a sales rep should have a good grasp on what responses they give to overcome the common concerns they encounter.

However, some sales reps with unbelievable potential may need several more weeks to get acclimated to the door-to-door environment. But just because a sales rep is slow to learn doesn't mean they should hang up their walking shoes just yet. I have witnessed numerous sales reps taking four to six weeks to start feeling comfortable on the doors, and they've turned out to be some of the top producers in their office.

In 2000, Rob G. was a rookie sales rep in Albuquerque, New Mexico. He had two weeks of experience under his belt but not a sale to show for it. To add insult to injury, the other seven sales reps in Rob's office had each sold at least three accounts—even the sales rep with the obnoxious lisp and receding hairline. Rob was seriously considering quitting the door-to-door sales job and returning home to work for his dad at the family's truck parts store. However, Rob was determined to keep the commitment he had made to himself and his manager and also to prove that he was capable of figuring out something that was proving to be quite challenging.

The next week Rob put in a few more hours on the doors than what he had normally been working and ended up selling his first two accounts. He continued putting in extra hours each week, and the next three weeks he sold nine, ten, and sixteen accounts respectively. Rob's confidence level was at an all-time high as he had figured out what he wanted to say and when he wanted to say it. He didn't doubt that no matter what a potential customer said to him, he would be able to respond commendably. And at the end of the sales season, Rob had become the top rookie sales rep in his office—much to the balding lisper's chagrin.

Rob's journey into the world of door-to-door sales didn't stop there. He continued as a successful sales rep for three more years. His door-to-door abilities paved his way to becoming a branch manager for a reputable pest-control company in the Midwest. After several years, Rob's branch became the flagship of the company, and in 2013, after more than a decade working in the pest-control industry, Rob became the chief operating officer of one of the top one hundred pest control companies in the nation. And to think, none of this would have come to fruition if Rob had decided the door-to-door sales business wasn't for him after two short weeks on the job.

Every sales rep is unique in terms of the length of time it will take them to overcome the learning curve. But no matter how long it takes, sales reps should monitor their progression by small improvements that are made from day to day, and in some cases from door to door. Sales reps should never compare themselves to others who might be enjoying success while they are mired in their own learning curve deficiencies. Patience is a must because success will come as sales reps remain dedicated and desire to make improvements. By working hard and working smart, every sales rep can convince potential customers to buy their product or service, even if that person has never before considered doing so. And when that happens, the sales rep has made it. They've become a successful door-to-door salesperson.

Appendix A

How to Effectively Get Rid of Door-to-Door Salespeople

At some point, most everybody will be approached by a door-to-door salesperson. As I've had the opportunity to approach thousands of people on their doorsteps, there have only been a small percentage that I have respected even though they declined my offer. Granted, as door-to-door sales reps, we realize we are uninvited guests and would never expect a red carpet to be rolled out when we arrive; however, salespeople don't deserve to be treated as infidels. We don't expect to sell everybody we talk to, but we do expect to be treated with courtesy by everybody we talk to. I thought it would be helpful to share some pointers on how to tactfully get rid of us door-to-door salespeople without being jerks about it.

Don't hide from us. We know you're in there.

Keep in mind that most door-to-door sales reps keep a log of every house they knock, and if you don't answer your door the first time, it's likely we will keep coming back until you do. So if you're in your house, answer the door.

It's frustrating when there are obvious signs of life in the house, but when the door is knocked or the doorbell rung, the house goes silent. It's especially annoying when this happens and you hear, "Shhhh," coming from inside the house. Just because you don't answer the door this time around doesn't mean we won't try again. Face the music; we know you're in there, so come out and talk to us. We don't bite.

Don't lie to us.

As door-to-door sales reps, we are acclimated to rejection. We don't take it personally, so if you don't want what we are offering, just be straight up about it. Don't make up excuses that aren't valid, or we'll continue to try and resolve your concerns, which wastes your time and ours. Just tell us like it is, and if you aren't a good candidate for what we are offering, we'll leave—no hard feelings.

But when you lie to us, you insult our intelligence and shame yourself. Remember, we are trained to recognize verbal and nonverbal signs that indicate whether people are being honest. If you are lying, we will probably continue to prod and probe just to annoy you. Honesty is the best policy when dealing with us.

Don't tell your kids to lie to us.

A young boy that couldn't have been more than five years old once told me that his mom and dad weren't home and that I should come back later. Not believing the boy, I asked him, "Go ask your mom when she will be home."

He then walked over to the stairway and yelled upstairs, "Mom, when will you be home?"

Come on, people. Asking your kids to lie for you? That's not right. By doing so, you set a dangerous precedent and damage your self-respect. An upstanding person will come to the door and talk to a salesperson like a grown-up.

Be respectful and we'll go away nicely.

As door-to-door sales reps, we will appreciatively walk away from your home when you treat us with respect. After we give our initial approach, a respectful response might be:

"Thanks for stopping by. I appreciate how hard you are working, but I'm not going to buy anything from you today, but I hope you have success with my neighbors. Can I get your phone number so if I ever have a need to buy what you are selling, I can contact you?"

This straightforward and respectful reply is virtually impossible to contend with because it communicates the respect that we as sales reps expect from everybody we contact. It also leaves open the possibility of a future sale, which ensures our shared respect.

"No $" works.

My wife is a bit of a pushover when it comes to buying from door-to-door sales reps. Because she's quite familiar with the challenges of the job, she tends to buy whatever is being sold. After she had purchased a window-washing service, two magazine subscriptions, and a lawn-care service in the span of four weeks, I figured I'd better educate her on how to reject sales reps' offers before she bankrupted us.

From my vast experience of being turned down on the doors, I've found the most difficult concern to overcome is when potential customers tell me they can't afford what I'm selling. Unless I'm willing to put money in their wallet, I haven't discovered an effective way to contest that concern. Of course, I would hope when this concern is given, the person is being honest.

If a potential customer politely tells me, "I appreciate you coming by the house, but at this time we don't have the money to spend on what you are selling. But you can try again in the future," there is nothing I can say that will convince them that my product or service is worth spending money that they don't have to spend.

We as sales reps are people too. We have feelings and emotions that can be hurt just like everybody else. We have our good days and bad days, and at the end of the day we want to be treated with the same respect we offer.

Being a door-to-door sales rep is not an easy job. Having to put our best foot forward at every contact is extremely challenging when everybody is saying, "no." But the "no's" are easier to digest and our days are more pleasant when we talk with people who are honest and respectful.

Appendix B

For Fun

I thought it would be fun to share a few of the most memorable experiences I had while knocking doors. Having knocked on tens of thousands of doors, I have come across people at the most inopportune times. I think I've seen and heard just about everything while standing on potential customers' doorsteps.

- People answering the door completely naked? Check.
- People verbally abusing one another? Check.
- People physically abusing one another? Check.
- People talking to themselves? Check.
- People singing to themselves? Check.
- People singing out of tune to themselves? Check.
- People dancing? Check.
- People dancing without rhythm? Check.
- People intoxicated? Check.

- People vomiting? Check.
- People cursing? Check.

Taking into account everything I've witnessed, a few personal experiences are so unique and unforgettable that they must be shared. So here for your enjoyment are a few of my most entertaining experiences while knocking doors as a door-to-door salesman:

Lil' Wayne

I'm not awestruck in the presence of celebrities. At the end of the day, they're just people who have developed a particular skill that others find impressive or important. However, during my door-knocking days, I did encounter (well, *almost* encountered, in one instance) two celebrities that I admired in one sense or another.

While selling pest-control contracts in New Orleans, Louisiana, my sales manager found out where Lil' Wayne, the famous rapper, lived. My manager claimed he had accidentally stumbled across the location of the home, but I believe he was being proactive in finding out where the rap superstar lived. Nonetheless, I was thrilled when my manager invited me to go with him to see if his sources had given him the correct location.

Lil' Wayne lived in a gated community in the suburbs of New Orleans, so as we drove from our office, we devised a strategy for talking the security guards into letting us into the private community. And, in the event our plan was foiled, we also planned an escape route.

We were driving a company truck and planned on telling the security guards that we had accidentally left a bulb duster at one of our customers' homes. Then we'd find Lil' Wayne's house, and I'd knock on his door while my manager video recorded the whole thing. What could go wrong?

As we approached the gated entrance, our idea seemed adolescent at best and we started to doubt our plan. Nevertheless, we summoned up the courage and my manager confidently told the security guard that we needed to retrieve our bulb duster that we had forgotten at a customer's home earlier in the week.

The guard was reluctant to let us enter the premises and told us that he would call our customer and have them bring the bulb duster to the front gate. Fortunately, my sales manager was quick to respond, "We already called and talked to them earlier. They aren't home right now but told us they'd leave the bulb duster on their porch for us."

My manager proceeded. "Listen, if I don't get this duster back, my manager will deduct the cost of a new one from my paycheck. Just let us in. We won't be long."

The security guard must have sensed my manager's desperation, because he agreed to open the gate and let us in. With the first step completed, we drove through the curving roads lined with gigantic mansions in search of Lil' Wayne's residence. Admittedly, intimidation began to set in as I viewed the size of these homes. I had knocked the doors of some large homes before, but these homes were the size of my elementary school.

It didn't take long until Lil' Wayne's house was in our sites. We knew what it looked like because it was the same home that was featured in his music video "Way of Life." My manager parked the truck across the street, got the video camera ready, and wished me luck.

As I walked up the driveway, I noticed two customized PT Cruiser limousines parked on the front lawn along with bullet bikes, four-wheelers, and other motorized toys. The house, yard, and vehicles looked almost identical to what had appeared in the music video, sans the partiers in sports jerseys and bikinis.

As I tried to maintain some level of professionalism, I was soaking in the fact that I was about to knock on the front door of Lil' Wayne's mansion. Before I knocked on the door, I checked with my manager to make sure he was recording. He gave me the thumbs-up, so I proceeded to ring the doorbell—except for one small problem: the doorbell was glued down and wouldn't ring. This must have been some kind of rapper trick to keep people like me from disturbing them. Nevertheless, I would not be dissuaded and proudly knocked on the massive door and then anxiously awaited an answer. But to my dismay, no sounds came from inside the home, and when I knocked again, I heard only the empty echo of my knock.

My guess was that Lil' Wayne was either still sleeping from a late night of partying or possibly hadn't returned home for the same reason. Needless to say I wasn't going to be selling a pest-control service to Lil' Wayne. But at least I have a great story to tell and video evidence to prove it.

Fennis Dembo

I may have struck out at Lil' Wayne's house, but that wasn't the case at Fennis Dembo's. If you aren't familiar with the name Fennis Dembo, you probably don't have a rooting interest in the University of Wyoming or the Detroit Pistons. Fennis was drafted by the Pistons with the thirtieth overall pick in the 1988 draft. His one and only season in the NBA was a championship year for the Pistons in 1989. He was rewarded with a championship ring even though he only averaged one point and less than one rebound per game.

He played his best basketball during his college years at the University of Wyoming. At the 1997 NCAA Tournament, he led the Cowboys to the Sweet Sixteen and was the leading scorer in the tournament, averaging nearly twenty-eight points a game. He finished his career at Wyoming as their all-time leading scorer and rebounder.

As a twelve-year-old I remember getting the *Sports Illustrated* with Fennis pictured on the cover dressed up in a cowboy hat, boots, and a lasso around his shoulder. The issue was titled "A Dazzling Dude…Wyoming's Fabulous Fennis Dembo." In fact, Fennis was the first-ever basketball player from the University of Wyoming to be featured on the cover of *Sports Illustrated*.

I never imagined meeting Fennis Dembo while knocking doors in Irondale, Alabama, but that's exactly what happened—even though I initially had no idea it was him. As I approached his midsized home, I was caught off guard as I witnessed this tall man standing on his front porch with a squirt bottle of bug killer in hand, literally reaching into the eaves of his house to spray a wasp nest.

Being that I was selling a pest-control service, I probably didn't give too much attention to his height and reach because I was more concerned about selling the service to a potential customer who had a pest problem. After my initial approach, he invited me to come into his home and tell him more about what I was offering. After a few more minutes of conversation, he agreed to sign up for the service.

I began the process of completing the information on the service agreement and asked him, "So what is your first name?"

To which he replied, "Fennis."

Then I said, "You mean like Fennis Dembo, the basketball player?"

He replied, "Yep, that's right."

Then I regrettably asked, "What's the last name I should put your account under?"

He looked at me with a smirk on his face and answered, "Dembo."

At that moment the picture of Fennis on the cover of the *Sports Illustrated* and the face of the man sitting in front of me collided, and I realized I was sitting at the kitchen table with *the* Fennis Dembo.

Completely embarrassed, I apologized for not recognizing him. We then went on to talk for several minutes about his career at the University of Wyoming. He was extremely gracious and even took me downstairs to show me his *Sports Illustrated* cover, framed and hanging on his basement wall. I will forever be a fan of #34.

Tornados in Tulsa

While training sales reps on the doors, I keep a tight schedule. The more efficient I am, the more time I am able to spend with each sales rep. I will routinely skip meals and bathroom breaks if for some reason I fall behind schedule. And in 2006, not even a tornado warning could keep me from sticking to my agenda.

I was in Tulsa, Oklahoma, and I had one more sales rep to knock with before I would be leaving to a different office the next morning. McKay, my business partner, and personal chauffeur while I was training sales reps, drove me to Spencer C., and despite the rain and wind, we began knocking doors. Shortly thereafter, tornado sirens began screaming throughout the city, but Spencer assured me this had been a common occurrence as of late and that they were only "warning sirens," so we continued knocking doors. Then, out of nowhere, we noticed McKay driving down the road toward us honking his horn and yelling at us to get in the car because he had heard on the radio that a tornado was heading our way.

I was determined to give Spencer a good training session, so I told McKay we were going to knock one more door before heading for cover with him. We hurried up to the next house and knocked on the door, and a large, burley man with a beard that would've made Grizzly Adams jealous looked at us as if we were crazy and exclaimed in a panic, "What are you doing out here? Tornado comin'. I'm gettin' in my hide-e-ho!"

He slammed the door in our faces, leaving us speechless. I certainly couldn't count that as my last door with Spencer, so I motioned to McKay that we were going next door for one more approach. The homeowners of this home were also in a bit of a panic, and upon opening the door, the wife proclaimed, "There is a tornado just a few miles from here! You better come inside with us if you don't have anywhere else to go."

We declined her offer, and knowing that the conditions weren't conducive to knocking doors, we raced back to the car, and McKay drove us to the nearest shopping center to take cover. We found our way into a Lowe's Home Improvement store, where an employee rushed us to the back of the store into a room where several others were hunkered down.

We nervously waited in the room for about twenty minutes and were cleared to leave once the weather service reported that our location was out of the tornado's trajectory. McKay drove us back to the neighborhood we had departed, and I was able to finish my training session with Spencer. I'm still not sure if knocking doors during a tornado warning is a sign of dedication or stupidity—but it's probably a little of both.

You can be the next Door-to-Door Millionaire by working directly with Lenny Gray!

His company, Rove Pest Control, is always looking to hire and partner with door-to-door sales reps and managers.

For more information, email Lenny at:
lennyg@d2dmillionaire.com

Visit his website at:
lennygray.com

Bibliography

Allen, Paul. *Idea Man: A Memoir by the Cofounder of Microsoft*. Portfolio, 2011.

BGR. "Black Friday Sales Top $1 Billion Online, Cyber Monday Expected To Set Record." Accessed November 26, 2012. http://bgr.com/2012/11/26/black-friday-sales-2012-cyber-monday-record/.

Business Week. "Sales Hits the Big Time at B-Schools." Accessed August 13, 2012. http://www.businessweek.com/articles/2012-08-13/sales-hits-the-big-time-at-b-schools.

CNN. "Violence mars Black Friday." Accessed November 26, 2011. http://edition.cnn.com/2011/11/25/business/money-black-friday-incidents/index.html.

CNN Money. "Black Friday sales hit record, says report." Accessed November 26, 2011. http://money.cnn.com/2011/11/26/pf/black_friday_sales/index.htm?iid=HP_LN.

—."Black Friday weekend: Record $52.4 billion spent." Accessed November 27, 2011. http://money.cnn.com/2011/11/27/pf/black_friday/index.htm.

Forbes. "Bill Gates." Last modified December 2012. http://www.forbes.com/profile/bill-gates/.

—."The World's Most Powerful People." Last modified December 5, 2012. http://www.forbes.com/powerful-people/.

Hogan, Kevin, and Ron Stubbs. *Can't Get Through: Eight Barriers to Communication*. Pelican, 2003.

HowStuffWorks. "Why is the Iowa caucus so important?" Accessed October 24, 2012. http://people.howstuffworks.com/iowa-caucus.htm.

Isaacson, Walter. *Steve Jobs*. Simon & Schuster, 2011.

Miller, Larry H., and Doug Robinson. *Driven: An Autobiography*. Deseret Book, 2012.

Monson, Thomas S. "See Others as They May Become," *Ensign*, November 2012, 70.

Napoleon Dynamite. DVD. Directed by Jared Hess. 2004; Beverly Hills, CA: Fox Searchlight Pictures, Paramount Pictures, 2004.

NY Daily News. "Worker dies at Long Island Wal-Mart after being trampled in Black Friday stampede." Accessed November 28, 2008. http://articles.nydaily-news.com/2008-11-28/local/17910475_1_wal-mart-worker-long-island-wal-mart-jdimytai-damour.

Orange County Register. "Poll: Which is least trusted profession?" Accessed May 23, 2010. http://jan.blog.ocregister.com/2010/05/23/poll-which-is-least-trusted-profession/37947/.

Possessions 2, *Notre Dame Magazine*.

Sales & Marketing Business Brief. "Sales no longer least trusted profession—but guess what is." Accessed May 31, 2010. http://www.businessbrief.com/sales-no-longer-least-trusted-profession-but-guess-what-is/.

Time. "TIME 100 Persons Of The Century." Last modified June 14, 1999. http://www.time.com/time/magazine/article/0,9171,991227,00.html.

United States Census Bureau. "Oklahoma." Last modified January 10, 2013. http://quickfacts.census.gov/qfd/states/40000.html.

Wikipedia. "Fennis Dembo." Last modified December 8, 2012. http://en.wikipedia.org/wiki/Fennis_Dembo.

—. "Homewood, Alabama." Last modified February 12, 2013. http://en.wikipedia.org/wiki/Homewood,_Alabama.

—. "Iowa caucuses." Last modified December 11, 2012. http://en.wikipedia.org/wiki/Iowa_caucuses.

—. "Keeping up with the Joneses." Last modified February 11, 2013. http://en.wikipedia.org/wiki/Keeping_up_with_the_Joneses.

—. "Lester Hayes." Last modified December 29, 2012. http://en.wikipedia.org/wiki/Lester_Hayes.

—. "Seinfeld." Last modified February 25, 2013. http://en.wikipedia.org/wiki/Seinfeld.

—. "Shooting the messenger." Last modified January 25, 2013. http://en.wikipedia.org/wiki/Shooting_the_messenger.

Made in the USA
Monee, IL
16 July 2022

99838990R00152